Not Peace but a Sword

The Case Against Early Christian Pacifism

Robert M. Price

I0805515

PITCHSTONE PUBLISHING
DURHAM, NORTH CAROLINA

Pitchstone Publishing
www.pitchstonebooks.com

Copyright © 2026 by Robert M. Price

Library of Congress Cataloging-in-Publication Data

Names: Price, Robert M., 1954- author
Title: Not peace but a sword : the case against early Christian pacifism / Robert M. Price.
Description: Durham, North Carolina : Pitchstone Publishing, [2025] | Includes bibliographical references. | Summary: "It has become a near-universal assumption that Jesus was a kind of first-century Mahatma Gandhi, a courageous champion of Pacifism and non-violent resistance. Likewise, everyone seems to agree that the Early Church was pacifistic. But for many years a few maverick scholars have made the case for Jesus having been an armed insurrectionist. In Not Peace but a Sword, Robert M. Price carries this "Jesus the Zealot" hypothesis significantly further and makes the case that Christians did not renounce "the sword of the Lord" even when Jesus was crucified as the "King of the Jews.""— Provided by publisher.
Identifiers: LCCN 2025020727 (print) | LCCN 2025020728 (ebook) | ISBN 9781634312868 paperback | ISBN 9781634312875 ebook
Subjects: LCSH: Pacifism—Religious aspects—Christianity—History of doctrines—Early church, ca. 30-600 | Violence—Religious aspects—Christianity—History of doctrines—Early church, ca. 30-600 | Peace—Biblical teaching | Violence—Biblical teaching | Church history—Primitive and early church, ca. 30-600
Classification: LCC BT736.6 .P75 2025 (print) | LCC BT736.6 (ebook)
LC record available at https://lccn.loc.gov/2025020727
LC ebook record available at https://lccn.loc.gov/2025020728

Not Peace but a Sword

CONTENTS

Introduction: Not Peace but a Sword[1]

One commonly reads that "the" earliest Christians[2] were steadfast pacifists and that in this they were simply following the teaching and example of their Lord, Jesus Christ. This book will seek to demonstrate that these beliefs are very far from being historically secure. But first it is worthwhile to call attention to the fact that this argument for Christian pacifism is most often put forth by sects descended from (or inspired by) the Radical Reformation movement: Anabaptists, Mennonites, Amish, Hutterites, Dunkers, Church of the Brethren, and Quakers (Society of Friends). It is of a piece with the fundamental self-understanding of these Protestant groups, all of whom see themselves as reversing the "Fall of the Church," the official legitimization

1. Matthew 10:34–36.

2. "[T]he important point for us to notice just now is, not only that ***the*** early Christians considered themselves bound by these precepts of love and non-resistance in an extremely close and literal way, but that they did actually interpret them as ruling out the indictment of wrongdoers in the law-courts and participation in the acts of war." (Cecil John Cadoux, *The Early Christian Attitude to War: A Contribution to the History of Christian* Ethics (London: Headley Brothers, 1919), p. 67. Emphasis mine.

of Christianity, the establishment of "Christendom," wrought by the Roman emperors Constantine and Theodosius. Protestants (and some others) claim that it was only then that Christ's cross-bearing soldiers began enlisting instead as sword-bearing soldiers of Caesar. (Nor were these the only moral compromises entailed in the devil's bargain with Caesar.)

There is a crucial irony in this scenario. Like Mormons, Plymouth Brethren, and Campbellites (Restorationists), their modern heirs take for granted what historians call the Hegesippian (or Eusebian)[3] model of Christian history: Jesus taught the orthodox creed to his apostles, who then indoctrinated the bishops they appointed as their successors, who in turn catechized the next generation likewise. Somewhere along the line, Satan muddied the waters by sending heretical infiltrators (Simon Magus, Marcion, Valentinus, Basilides, Bardesanes, Satornilus, Carpocrates, et. al.) with their fantastic yet seductive distortions of the true gospel of Christ. But for some time now, critical historians have realized that this is not at all the way it must have happened. And that means the Christian pacifism argument is flawed insofar as it depends on the old model of a unitary, pure and original "Early Church."

Of course, these ancient churchmen realized there were dissenting Christian voices against which Origen, Tertullian, Lactantius, et. al., polemicized. There were Christians who were happy to go to the recruitment centers. But these are treated as excuse-making Christian compromisers who had no business joining (or remaining in) the ranks of the Roman military. There is no attempt to reconstruct the possible ethical doctrine allow-

---

3. Two early Christian historians.

ing "Christian soldiering." Justin already speaks of numerous self-described "Christians" (sects of Marcion, Valentinus, Basilides, etc.) who do not follow what *he* considers the teaching of Jesus, which obviously they didn't so regard.

Many Lords, Many Faiths, Many Baptisms

F.C. Baur[4] was the first to notice how much of the New Testament makes sense only once you realize there was a major conflict between two rival Christianities, one Jewish in orientation, led by Simon Peter, and the other Gentile, led by Paul. The first kept the Jewish Law and saw Jesus as a nationalistic Messiah. The second saw the Law as passé and understood Jesus in an internationalized, "spiritualized" way. Most of the New Testament writings lined up on either side of this great divide, and the rest were part of a later effort to paper over the differences once the two factions had buried the hatchet and merged into Catholic orthodoxy. Baur recognized, for instance, that Matthew's gospel directs its readers to observe strictly every last regulation of the Torah (5:17–19) and condemns those ostensible Christians who don't (7:21–23, "Depart from me, you who practice lawlessness!"). Paul and his followers must be in view here. The Epistle of James has Paul in its sites, too ("You fool! Do you want to be shown that faith apart from works is dead?" 2:20, after which follows a refutation of the Pauline Romans 3:27–4:1–5ff.) On the other hand, in Galatians and 2 Corinthians Paul lambasts

4. Ferdinand Christian Baur, *The Church History of the First Three Centuries*. Vol. I. Trans. Allan Menzies. Theological Translation Fund Library (Williams and Norgate, 1878).

certain "super-apostles" who require Gentile, Pauline converts to "Judaize" (2 Cor. 11:4–5, 13–15: Gal. 1:6–9; 2:14). Paul claims that they represent a false gospel message designed by Satan. Mark's gospel sides with Paul in affirming that Jesus swept away all kosher laws (7:19), an editorial comment that Law-loving Matthew clipped when he appropriated that section of Mark into his own later gospel (compare Matt. 15:17). Jewish Torah-Christians like Matthew venerated Peter and the Twelve, whose number obviously stood for the twelve tribes of Israel. Paul, as we have seen, had little regard for these men. Mark followed Paul in this, too, portraying the disciples of Jesus as blithering idiots every chance he got. Baur placed Revelation, with its reverence for "the twelve apostles of the Lamb" (21:14) and for the twelve "tribes of the sons of Israel" (7:4–8; 21:12), in the column with Matthew and James, while the Gospel and Epistles of John, together with Hebrews, belonged in the Pauline camp.

Representing the later stage of reconciliation were Luke's gospel and its sequel, the Acts of the Apostles, as well as 1 and 2 Peter and 1 and 2 Timothy and Titus. Acts parallels Peter and Paul, having each apostle preach the same message and perform identical miracles: miraculous jailbreaks (Acts 12:1–11; 16:23–26), healing by articles of clothing (5:14–16; 19:11–12), raising the dead (9:36–42; 20:7–12), restoring the lame (3:1–8; 14:8–10), squaring off with magicians (8:9–24; 13:6–11). The Twelve are honored, but so is Paul. And though Luke seems to put the Twelve on a slightly higher level, he spends most of his narrative on the perils of Paul. No fan of either figurehead, Peter or Paul, reading Luke's Acts could come away with his hostility to the other apostle left intact. Likewise, the pseudepigraphical Epistles of Peter present a Peter who, in 1 Peter, sounds like Paul (so much so, in fact, that many scholars today think the writer of 1 Peter copied from the Pauline Epistle to the Ephesians!), and who, in 2 Peter, mentions Paul by name, calling him "blessed" so long as one doesn't interpret his writings in a heretical fashion (3:15–16). Thus Luke-Acts and 1 and 2 Peter, Baur said, are "catholicizing" in their tendency, just like the later church legends which make Peter and Paul a kind of dynamic duo working together to found the church at Rome. Ditto for the whole notion that the Twelve fanned out across the known world preaching the gospel. Paul's letters make it clear that he, not they, was the one and only Apostle to the Gentiles (Gal. 2:7–9; Rom. 1:5, 14; 15:15–20). Later legend remodeled the Twelve, originally the governors of Jewish Christians in Palestine (Matt. 19:28, "You shall sit on twelve thrones, governing the twelve tribes of Israel."), in the image of the jet-setting Paul.

I believe much, even most, of Baur's reconstruction is still persuasive, as far as it went. There was, however, more to say, and Walter Bauer[5] said a lot of it. He jumped up into the second century. By reexamining just about every scrap of evidence surviving from the period, Bauer uncovered a remarkable fact: it turned out that in several major segments of the Mediterranean world the first kind of Christianity to set up shop and hang out the shingle was not what we know as Catholic orthodoxy at all, but rather one or another variety of so-called heresy. On this or that frontier of Christian expansion "Christianity" simply meant Marcionism, Ebionism, Encratism, Gnosticism. The resultant picture, of course, was antipodal to the traditional version of

5. Walter Bauer, *Orthodoxy and Heresy in Earliest Christianity*. Trans, Philadelphia Seminar on Christian Origins (Philadelphia: Fortress Press, 1971).

Eusebius, Constantine's apologist and pet theologian, whereby "heresy" had appeared only after the apostles had planted Catholic orthodoxy all over the Roman Empire.

Walter Bauer began his demonstration of the artificiality of this scenario by focusing on Edessa, a major center of early Christianity in eastern Syria. He showed how the Chronicle of Edessa records as events of note the births or arrivals of Marcion, Bardesanes, and Mani before it ever gets around to mentioning the establishment of a church building by representatives of orthodoxy. Eusebius himself has nothing to say of any early orthodox Christianity in the area, though he cannot help mentioning the early ministry of Bardesanes and the circulation there of the *Diatessaron* of Tatian (a compilation of Matthew, Mark, Luke, John, and a bit of Thomas into a single narrative), which Eusebius considered heretical.

Justin Martyr and heresiologists preserved the embarrassing fact that the name "Christian" in Edessa was the exclusive property of the Marcionites, and that the apparently late-arriving orthodox had to be satisfied with being called "Palutians" after the first orthodox Edessan bishop, Palut. In fact, this remained the state of affairs until the Muslim conquest! A note from contemporary Greater Armenia makes clear that "heretics" were in the vast majority in the region. In light of these facts, Bauer deduced that the famous apocryphal correspondence between King Abgarus of Edessa and Jesus (in which the king, having heard of Jewish plots on Jesus' life, invites him to take refuge in Edessa), must have originated as a spurious pedigree for apostolic orthodoxy in Edessa, as if dating back already to the time of Jesus himself and his apostle Addai (Thaddaeus) whom he sent to Abgarus with his "Thanks, but no thanks" reply.

Helmut Koester (more about whom in a moment) has supplemented Bauer's argument by locating the Thomas tradition (The Gospel of Thomas, Acts of Thomas, Book of Thomas the Contender, etc.) in Eastern Syria. This means that the "heretical" tendencies in the region go back very early indeed, perhaps even to the apostle Thomas himself, whom tradition says missionized the region.

In Western Syria, Antioch especially, we see a similar picture. Antioch is already pictured as a major center of Christian mission activity in Acts and Galatians. Paul, Peter, and Matthew are all associated with Antioch. Whether they were representatives of what would later be known as Catholic orthodoxy depends on how one interprets their writings (as well as which writings attributed to them one thinks are authentic!). The first post-biblical missions we know of in Western Syria were those of the Gnostics Satornilus/Saturninus, Cerdo, and Menander. It is in this region also that we find the orthodox bishop Serapion in 190 CE condemning the widespread usage of the local favorite Gospel of Peter, which he deemed Docetic[6] and heretical. When we get to the Letters of Ignatius, which Bauer considered authentic (at least the seven so received today), we must infer that Ignatius' desperate pleading for the firm control of, and absolute obedience to, the bishop in each church denotes a power struggle against a flood of "heresies" (docetic and Judaizing) which only an iron-handed authoritarianism could hope to quash. Similarly, the Epistle of Polycarp (which, again, Bauer considered authentic) laments that "the great majority"

---

6. "Docetism," from the Greek *dokeo*, "to seem," held that Jesus was never really incarnated, i.e., in solid flesh, but was like an angel or a phantom.

embrace Docetism. Ignatius writes to Polycarp, and not to all his brother bishops, but rather only to those who take his side in the struggle, implying a real diversity of views. In all this we need not infer a falling away from a prior orthodoxy. It may just as well imply a first serious attempt of orthodoxy to establish the dominance that it would eventually secure.

In Asia Minor we need only look at some late New Testament writings to discover an early, pervasive presence of "heresy." The Book of Revelation (Apocalypse of John) depicts a struggle between two parties, neither of which would qualify as orthodox by later standards. John the Revelator represents a type of ascetical Christianity (it is only 144,000 "virgins who have not defiled themselves with women" who will be saved, 14:4), and his bitter enemies, to be found throughout the seven churches under John's jurisdiction, are the Gnostic sect of the Nicolaitans.

In Acts and the Pastoral Epistles (quite likely all the work of one author)[7] we have the strategic admission made pseudonymously through the lips of "Paul" that "All Asia has turned against me" (2 Tim. 1:15) and that "after my departure savage wolves will come in among you, not sparing the flock" of the Ephesian church (Acts 20:29). In other words, these catholicizing sources make the best of the fact that Paul's ministry in Asia Minor was not succeeded by Catholic orthodoxy. Of course, the assumption is that Paul must have taught orthodox views, so Luke can understand the state of things in his day (the second century) only as the result of an apostasy from Pauline purity.

Egypt presents us with the same picture yet again. The first attested workers for Christ there were the Gnostics Valentinus,

---

7. Stephen G. Wilson, *Luke and the Pastoral Epistles* (London: SPCK, 1979).

Basilides, Apelles, Carpocrates, and his son Isidore. Phlegon preserves a letter attributed to Hadrian noting that all Christian priests in Egypt worshipped Serapis, too! The leading gospels in Egypt, the Gospels according to the Hebrews and according to the Egyptians, as far as we can tell from the extant fragments, were Gnostic or heretical in color. Bauer could detect no trace of orthodoxy in Egypt until the third century bishop Demetrius. But does not tradition make the gospel writer Mark the first bishop of Egypt? Indeed, it does, but like the Letters of Jesus and Abgarus, this legend seems to be but another spurious retroactive pedigree meant to fabricate an "orthodox" origin for Egyptian Christianity (assuming Mark and his gospel could themselves be judged orthodox!).

Bauer lived to see his portrait of Egyptian Christianity amply confirmed by the discovery in 1948 of the Nag Hammadi library, a cache of Gnostic gospels, epistles, tracts, and revelations which revealed an astonishing diversity of Christian beliefs the breadth of which not even Bauer had dared suspect! Who would have guessed that Sethian Gnostics had become Christians on the assumption that Jesus was the reincarnation of Seth or of Melchizedek? Or that Jesus was believed in some quarters to have been the reincarnation of "the Illuminator," Zoroaster? What makes this discovery all the more astonishing is that associated documents show the collection of leather-bound volumes to have been taken from the monastic library of the Brotherhood of Saint Pachomius, the first Christian monastery we know of. Apparently, when the monks received the Easter Letter from Athanasius in 367, which contains the first known listing of the canonical 27 New Testament books, warning the faithful to read no others, the brethren must have decided to hide their cherished "heretical" gospels, etc., lest they fall into the hands of the ecclesiastical book-burners. We may perhaps take that monastery as a cameo, a microcosm, of Egyptian Christianity in the fourth century, diverse in doctrine, though soon to suffocate beneath the smothering veil of Catholic orthodoxy.

How did Catholic orthodoxy manage to dominate? Bauer saw Rome as central to this development. There is striking evidence for an early diversity of belief in the Roman church, including the traditions of Marcion and Valentinus being influential leaders there for a time (something absolutely impossible if Rome had then shared the same view of these arch-heretics as later orthodoxy would). The Shepherd of Hermas, a writing widely considered Christian scripture, was the work of Hermas, the brother of bishop Pius of Rome (died 154), and it contains teachings scarcely characteristic of later Catholicism, especially as regards Jesus Christ. But eventually Catholic orthodoxy prevailed in Rome, and thanks to the emerging myth of apostolic succession, the bishops of Rome, with their spurious pedigree of joint Petrine-Pauline foundation, pulled rank.

Consolidated in the center of the empire, Catholic orthodoxy spread next to Corinth via the circulation of 1 and 2 Corinthians and 1 Clement (and if Harnack was right, 2 Clement, too, possibly written by the Roman bishop Soter). These letters invoked the authority of Paul to combat factionalism and Gnostic heresy in Corinth. By 100 CE the Corinthian bishop Dionysius was in Rome's pocket and began writing his own anti-heretical epistles to other churches. By the middle of the second century Roman influence extended to Hierapolis in Asia Minor (next door to the New Testament cities of Colossae and Laodicea), though it was by no means secure there. I suspect that another major tool of Roman propaganda was the Epistles of Ignatius, which like the earlier Tübingen School, but unlike Walter Bauer, I regard as spurious: they depict the Syrian bishop being "extradited" to Rome for execution for no apparent reason, against a rival tradition that he was killed at home in Syria. The real point, I think, was to account for the fact that these epistles were first received from Rome, not because Ignatius had been *taken* there and their delivery was delayed, but rather because they were *written* there in a later generation.

The strategy of the orthodox apologists was to defame instead of refute. Their mud-slinging against the Arians and the Montanists, for example, are both comical and grotesque. They simply assumed their own belief was the old, the original, faith, despite the fact that the Gnostics had their own claims to apostolic succession. Valentinus, for example, claimed to have received the teaching of Paul at the hands of the latter's disciple Theodas, while Basilides credited his teaching to Glaukias, the disciple of Simon Peter. Were orthodox claims necessarily better grounded than these? Both are equally likely to be fictitious. Eusebius and other heresiologists late-dated Marcion and other heretics and forged a genealogical chain of "heretical succession" whereby it would appear that all the troublemakers inherited their errors from one another along a narrow channel. The point of this was to make unorthodox ideas appear to be a late growth as well as the property of a few related eccentrics instead of the widespread credos of whole sections of Christendom. Likewise, Eusebius refers to a vast corpus of anti-heretical literature dating back to the second century, but he actually cites very little, implying he has falsely generalized from a very few specimens known to him (his method at many other points as well).

Why did Rome prevail? Why did Roman propaganda succeed? The orthodox had tighter organization. Among the heretics, the two movements who did organize into congregations, the second-century Marcionites and the third-century Manichean Gnostics, flourished all over the empire and beyond until they were exterminated within Rome's boundaries and died away slowly elsewhere. Most Gnostics existed as secretive cells within larger Catholic congregations and were forced to leave or keep quiet. Gnostics in general were fissiparous and free-thinking. They were not the type to forge and enforce a single orthodoxy. Encouraging individual spiritual exploration, they were not great institution-builders. Many banded together on the model of the ancient philosophical schools, circles of disciples gathered around a teacher. Such is not the stuff of mass movements.

Also, Catholic orthodoxy represented the lowest common denominator, stripped of both the subtleties and the drastic asceticism of the heresies. This meant it was easier for most people to grasp. Bauer might have appreciated the analogies provided today by the victory of fundamentalism in world Protestantism: simple-minded dogmatism is always more popular (as Dean Kelly showed in his *Why Conservative Churches Are Growing*).[8]

The theoretical constructions of Baur and Bauer, as wide-ranging and illuminating as they are, are each but pieces of a larger picture. Walter Bauer showed how Catholic orthodoxy triumphed over rivals no younger than itself, while F.C. Baur had tried to explain the origin of Catholic Christianity as the fusion of two prior factions (Judaizing, Petrine Christianity and

8. Dean M. Kelly, *Why Conservative Churches Are Growing: A Study in Sociology of Religion* (New York: Harper & Row, 1972).

Gentile, Pauline Christianity). The Pauline-Petrine compromise would then have become the victor over other Christian parties, like Gnostics and Encratites with whom Baur had been little concerned. Both Baur and Bauer seem to have underestimated the continuing importance of Jewish Christianity. It remained for other scholars, particularly Helmut Koester, James M. Robinson,[9] and Burton L. Mack[10] to fill out the picture Baur and Bauer had painted in sure but broad strokes.[11]

In short, we might compare the situation to that of today's agribusiness, whose lab-engineered mutant strains have squeezed out older "heirloom strains."

Yet hidden within the Christian pacifist argument is an even more damning irony. The very claim that "the early Christians" were all pacifists shares the false assumption that the "real" Christianity was the "Model A" version, not some later "Edsell" Christianity. Thus we find in the pacifist writings of Origen, Lactantius, Tertullian, and others the repeated insistence that "the" Christian stance toward Christian participation in the military was "Better dead than red." Dying as a refusenik was better than having to kill the enemies of Rome in battle. It can be no surprise to the historian that we have little to no expressions of the reasoning of those who saw no problem answering the call

---

9. James M. Robinson and Helmut Koester, *Trajectories through Early Christianity* (Philadelphia: Fortress Press, 1971).

10. Burton L. Mack, *A Myth of Innocence: Mark and Christian Origins* (Philadelphia: Fortress Press, 1988). See also, Robert M. Price, *Deconstructing Jesus* (Amherst: Prometheus Books, 2000), pp. 21–96, for my slight retooling of Mack's taxonomy of proto-Christianities.

11. It is surprising how much information still survives concerning these alternatives to "normative" Christianity. See M. David Litwa, *Found Christianities: Remaking the World of the Second Century CE* (London: T&T Clark, 2022).

when Uncle Constantine was looking for a few good men. After all, it was our "Patristic peaceniks" who had to bear the burden of proof, implying that military Christians had no qualms of conscience to rationalize away.

Gentle Jesus, Meek and Mild?

A second, equally problematic consideration is that the whole Christian pacifist case is premised on an (inferred) "official" portrait of Jesus that is similarly the product of second-century Catholicism, a highly selective and perhaps even bowdlerized, "sanitized" version of the Christian figurehead. A whole tradition of critical scholarship has arrived at one version or another of a very different Jesus character. Hermann Samuel Reimarus, Robert Eisler, and S.G.F. Brandon have reconstructed an alternative Jesus portrait that better explains the "anomalous data" (Thomas S. Kuhn)[12] of which the traditional Jesus characterization could make no plausible sense. According to this approach, the historical Jesus was a Zealot or Zealot-like armed revolutionist, and that, instead of abandoning their allegiance to the defeated rebel Messiah, his partisans switched to an Essene-like quietism in order to evade/forestall further Roman persecution. The resulting Jesus was only falsely accused as an anti-Roman seditionist but was a non-threatening, accommodationist of the same flavor as the Pharisees and Sadducees. We will explore this possibility at greater length later, but in the meantime, there is

12. Thomas S. Kuhn, *The Structure of Scientific Revolutions* (Chicago: University of Chicago Press, 1962).

an oft-neglected question we ought to raise: why should any recoverable political views we might ascribe to Jesus be considered normative—even for Christians?

Traditionally it has not been supposed that Jesus had anything quite like what we would call political opinions or beliefs. Orthodox Christians in fact did not picture Jesus as having any *opinions* on anything at all. You know the slogan: "The gospel is good *news*, not good *views*." Even so, as the earthly avatar of Jehovah, Jesus did not need "opinions," which are, by definition, less than certain, more tentative, like theories which compete with rival theories. What need had he for such gropings? After all, he did not see in a glass darkly but already face to face. And this contrast hints at a serious inconsistency underlying the whole endeavor to reconstruct "the politics of Jesus." On the one hand, we ask what this *man's* political opinions might be, as if we were asking after those of Ashley Judd or Sean Penn. On the other, we ask this because we imagine that, whatever views we may decide Jesus held, they will be normative for us, implying we consider them no mere opinions from which we may learn, but rather divine dictates which we may demand that others must join us in following. It is a case of theo-political bait-and-switch and, finally, of cynical manipulation. Since we cannot be certain of what political stance Jesus may have held, it must be sheer manipulation to choose one model and use it to command allegiance to the particular politics that one prefers. The only saying of Jesus I consider relevant to our topic is this one: "Why do you not decide for yourselves what is right?" (Luke 12:57). Don't take lazy short cuts. Consider the issues and to what extent your principles can be applied without adjustment to actual conditions. Where will you strike the balance between idealism and realism?[13] It takes work.

What's the alternative? If your approach is simply to obey Jesus in the gospels as if you were reading Chairman Mao's *Little Red Book*, you are begging the question of what he actually did teach. You will be making a false idol of whatever scholar who is using "Jesus" as a mouthpiece. You are allowing yourself to be manipulated. It's easier that way, after all.

But it is worse than that. Suppose you *could* be sure of Jesus' political views? And suppose you felt obligated to parrot them and obey them, come hell or high water? How would it not be theocratic fanaticism like that of radical Islam?

---

13. Reinhold Niebuhr, *An Interpretation of Christian Ethics* (New York: Living Age Books/Meridian Books, 1956), Chapter 4, "The Relevance of an Impossible Ethical Ideal," pp. 97–123.

1 The Sword of the Lord
Vestiges of Zealotry in the Gospels

Reimarus and the Rebel[1]

Was Jesus a violent revolutionist? I believe the first to propose this was the eighteenth-century Deist Hermann Samuel Reimarus.[2] He noted that the gospels clearly depict Jesus' disciples expecting an earthly regime to be headed by their Master. They jockeyed for positions of honor and power alongside him (Mark 9:33–34; 10:35–37). They expected the liberation of Israel from Roman rule (Luke 24:21; Acts 1:6).

> They quarreled about who would be greatest in this kingdom of heaven, and even though all twelve of them, to be sure, were to sit on twelve thrones to judge the twelve tribes of Israel, yet one of them wishes to sit at the right hand of Jesus the Messiah and another on the left. That is, they want to be next in importance to the Messiah and have the most to

1. With apologies to Colin Wilson and his book *Religion and the Rebel*.

2. Charles H. Talbert, ed., *Reimarus: Fragments*. Trans. Ralph S. Fraser. Lives of Jesus Series (Philadelphia: Fortress Press, 1970).

> say, bearing in their minds that this kingdom of God was to be revealed immediately. . . . Thus Jesus' disciples as heralds of the kingdom of heaven, not only on that occasion [Mark 6:7–13], but even long afterward, were thinking of a temporal kingdom of the Messiah. They proclaimed just this in all the cities, schools, and homes of Judea. Indeed and what is more, these apostles even after Jesus' death, speak in the same way of his intention and plan. "We had hoped that he (Jesus of Nazareth) was the one to redeem Israel" (Luke 24:21).[3]

Nor can we imagine he would not have drilled them on what they were to preach, to make sure they were correctly representing him (cf. 1 John 2:19). If subsequent to this we see the disciples continuing in their belief in a this-worldly regime for Jesus and themselves as his cronies, we have no right to believe Jesus taught anything different, i.e., some more "spiritual" version of the coming kingdom (contra John 18:36).

> As regards the sending out of the apostles on their mission, we must suppose, either that Jesus did or did not know what their impression of the kingdom of heaven was. In the first case, it is clear that his object must have been to rouse the Jews to the expectation of a speedy worldly deliverance, because he employed messengers whom he knew had no other belief, and therefore could not preach a different one. In the second case, if he did not know their impression, he must still have guessed them to be under the universally prevailing one, and so ought to have enlightened and instructed the disciples until they abandoned their delusion, and were fully convinced of the truth of his real object, in order that they might not propagate a false gospel. . . . Therefore he must have approved

3. Reimarus, p. 127.

> of the prevailing belief among the disciples and people, and it must have been his object to encourage and circulate it throughout Judea.[4]

But Jesus' planned revolution failed, and the disciples regrouped, transforming Christianity from a political movement to an otherworldly salvation cult. "We cannot believe otherwise than that the apostles of Jesus retained their previous aims and purposes, and sought to bring about their fulfillment as best they could, although in a different manner."[5] But what exactly *were* those aims and purposes? Reimarus describes the spiritualized reconception of the kingdom of God. And thus far what he proposes concerning this reformulation of Jesus' gospel message rings true to the analogy of what occurs every time a "Doomsday cult"[6] is forced by uncooperative events to dial back their eschatological enthusiasm, the deliteralizing of their failed prediction. "Oh, it happened all right, just not in the visible way we expected. The kingdom *has* come—if you, uh, have eyes to see it!" That is the stuff of cognitive dissonance.[7] But there are also numerous occasions where even the cult leaders cannot accept the face-saving strategy even while encouraging their followers to buy it. Thus is born a cynical hypocrisy that naturally leads to the shepherd fleecing the sheep. And Reimarus saw this happening in the wake of Jesus' death. And he did not merely tend

---

4. Reimarus, pp. 137–138.

5. Reimarus, p. 242.

6. John Lofland, *Doomsday Cult: A Study of Conversion, Proselytization and Maintenance of Faith* (Englewood Cliffs: Prentice Hall, 1966).

7. Leon Festinger, Henry W. Riecken, and Stanley Schachter, *When Prophecy Fails: A Social and Psychological Study of a Modern Group That Predicted the Destruction of the World* (New York: Harper & Row, Torchbook edition, 1964).

to think the worst of the apostles because he could not bring himself to believe in the miracles they proclaimed, in which case Peter, Andrew, and the rest *had* to be charlatans. No, remember how Reimarus had already cited ample proofs that the disciples of Jesus were, so to speak, already parting his garments among them before he ever got to Golgotha! "Who gets to be top man? Who gets the best seats? How many jewels in my crown, Lord?" In their Master's "tragic" death, they saw golden opportunities! And to realize them, the apostles had as little compunction about switching sides as did Captain Renault in *Casablanca*. Or Josephus, for that matter.

To this matter we shall presently turn. But we must at least momentarily consider the prime item of evidence that Reimarus was right in his diagnosis of the less than stellar motives of Jesus' self-aggrandizing successors, namely the scare-story of Ananias and Sapphira (Acts 5:1–11).[8] We are first informed that, in order to create a common relief fund for the needy among the believers, those who possessed property sold it and laid the proceeds at the feet of the apostles, already an ominous choice of words suggesting the spoils of conquest. Ananias and Sapphira covet the reputation of big givers like Joseph (Barnabas) of Cyrene

8. Alfred Loisy, *The Origins of the New Testament*. Trans. L.P. Jacks (London: George Allen and Unwin, 1950), p. 173: "Whatever may be the source of it, the hair-raising story of Ananias and Sapphira is another invention intended to exalt the prestige of apostolic and ecclesiastical authority." See also Luke Timothy Johnson, *The Literary Function of Possessions in Luke-Acts*. SBL Dissertation Series (Atlanta: Scholars Press, 1977). The story has been constructed from the stories of Achan (Joshua chapter 6) and of Naboth's Vineyard (1 Kings chapter 21), as per Thomas L. Brodie, "Luke the Literary Interpreter: Luke-Acts as a Systematic Rewriting and Updating of the Elijah-Elisha Narrative in 1 and 2 Kings." Rome: Pontifical University of St. Thomas Aquinas, 1981, chapter 5, "The Elijah-Elisha Text and Luke's Themes of the Fraudulent Couple and the Martyred Man," pp. 271–287.

and so sell some property, as he did, and conspicuously turn it over to the divine apostles. But they harbor certain suspicions as to the ultimate destination of the money (perhaps well-founded, as it turns out), so they keep back some of the money for a rainy day. Supernaturally informed of this perfidy, Peter exposes their deception and strikes them dead with the sword of his mouth. But are we to suppose that at least the money they did contribute ever made it to the poor? Perhaps not, as in the very next chapter we are told that the holy apostles are too busy preaching the gospel to squander their time on poor relief, so they delegate that job to newly-appointed subordinates—who are subsequently depicted as *also* preaching and evangelizing! It would be grossly unfair to generalize about the apostolic community from a single incident, but on the other hand it is evident that the author must consider the Ananias and Sapphira tale complementary to his church's reputation. Presumably, he is proud of it, not ashamed. It is *he*, not just Reimarus, who seeks to portray the church in this way.

Eyes on Eisler

Decades later, Robert Eisler[9] renewed this theory, appealing to the then-recently discovered Slavonic version of Josephus' *Jewish War*, which contains a longer version of the notorious *Testimonium Flavianum* which occurs instead in Josephus' other major Greek language book, *Jewish Antiquities*, in shorter compass.

9. Robert Eisler, *The Messiah Jesus and John the Baptist*. Trans. Alexander Haggerty Krappe (New York: Dial Press, 1931).

(This would be just one of many parallel passages shared by both the *Antiquities* and the *Jewish War*.) The Slavonic Josephus is a puzzling work. At least most scholars find it so, I think because the only conjecture that makes any sense would complicate things for them if they embraced it. That conjecture? If the text is a forgery from a previous era—why? Whose interests could have been served by it? It promotes no identifiable heresy. And way too much detail seems to serve no agenda at all, save to supply fuller accounts of events recounted more succinctly in the Greek Josephus. Rather, why not accept the document as it presents itself: a Slavonic translation of the lost Aramaic version of Josephus' *Wars of the Jews*. The Aramaic represented a different edition, any other language versions having perished. We know Josephus was in the habit of revising and updating his works, so none of this is particularly improbable.

The reason this is controversial is that the Slavonic Josephus features much expanded reports of John the Baptizer and Jesus (hence the title of Eisler's book). Eisler is/was not alone in questioning the dates of John the Baptist. Others have noted that Josephus' report that Herod Antipas' defeat at the hands of Aretas IV was popularly considered God's punishment for Antipas, who had executed the Baptizer for publicly denouncing Antipas' dumping Aretas' daughter to marry his brother's wife instead. But the defeat must have followed pretty soon after John's beheading if people were to connect the two events causally. But if so, then we'd have to place John's death some years *after* Jesus' crucifixion! Somebody seems to have got things confused somewhere along the line! But it gets worse: there is some reason to place John's public activities years *before* Jesus' public career. And here is where Eisler and the Slavonic Josephus come in.

The Slavonic version depicts John in terms familiar from his appearance in the New Testament gospels—but he is not actually *named*. Hauled before the authorities, he is asked to identify himself. All he answers is that "I am a man; as such has the spirit of God called me, and I live on bullrushes and roots and wood shavings."[10] Eisler suggests that, not only does his description match him with the baptizing Nazoreans/Mandeans, but his utterance "I am a man" looks like a theologically oblivious rendering of "I am Enosh," the angelic Power believed by Mandeans to have visited the earth in the form of John the Baptist! The Mandean *Book of John* also makes Jesus and John contemporaries (though it casts Jesus as a false messiah!).

From all this, Eisler very plausibly infers that John the Baptist was in fact active during the tenure of Archelaus, against whose persecuting wrath the angel sought to protect Jesus' father Joseph in Matthew 2:22–23. And John's activity was political, urging the Jews to join up with Judas of Galilee. Eisler, having lit this torch, then uses it to illuminate a puzzling passage in Matthew 11:11–15 (cf Luke 16:16):

> Truly, I say to you, among those born of women there has risen no one greater than John the Baptist; yet he who is least in the kingdom of heaven is greater than he. From the days of John the Baptist until now the kingdom of heaven has suffered violence, and men of violence take it by force. For all the prophets and the law prophesied until John; and if you are willing to accept it, he is Elijah who is to come. He who has ears to hear, let him hear.

---

10. Eisler, p. 225.

These verses are not haphazardly juxtaposed. Eisler notes that Jesus seems here to regard John and his ministry as belonging sometime in the remembered past: "From those days till now. . . ." And he implies that John inaugurated a well-known period of revolutionary activity. Otherwise why associate him with that period? It is cringe-inducing to read these verses as conservatives and fundamentalists try to evade the political coloring. "Oh," they say, "that only means that the gospel was making great progress because people were actively talking it up with their friends and neighbors." Diogenes must have been delighted to come upon apologist Clifford A. Wilson, who was honest enough to admit that the passage meant this:

> Possibly our Lord was suggesting that some were attempting to force the emergence of the Kingdom of God by *compelling* God to usher in His Kingdom in the special sense they hoped for. He went on to say that forceful men seize it—possibly referring to men such as the Zealots and the Sicarii (who were even more violently opposed to the rule of Rome).[11]

But, unlike Wilson, Eisler saw that the "forceful men" mentioned here must have been the Baptist's men! Eisler bids us take another look at the directions Luke has John the Baptist issue to those who came to him for baptism (as a rite of purification preparatory to holy war):

> And the multitudes asked him, "What then shall we do?" And he answered them, "He who has two coats, let him share with him who has none; and he who has food, let him do like-

11. Clifford A. Wilson, *New Light on the Gospels* (Grand Rapids: Baker Book House, 1970), p. 66.

> wise." Tax collectors also came to be baptized, and said to him, "Teacher, what shall we do?" And he said to them, "Collect no more than is appointed you." Soldiers also asked him, "And we, what shall we do?" And he said to them, "Rob no one by violence or by false accusation, and be content with your wages." (Luke 3:10–15)

Eisler notes that the word *strateuomenoi* denotes not simply "soldiers" (which would instead be *stratiotai*), but rather "those going off to war." These champions of the sole rule of Yahweh were commanded not to pillage the citizenry whose defenders, after all, they were supposed to be. Taxation would still be necessary, paid to the new, native government, but tax-collectors were told not to extort money beyond the actual sums owed. And the rebels were exhorted to share clothing with their comrades since obviously they had no government-issued clothing or weaponry. John, then, anticipated the rabble-rousing recruiting tactics of the bishops and pious hermits who whipped up the Medieval Crusades.[12]

If John's "forceful men" were armed revolutionaries, what about Jesus' lieutenants? The names and epithets of some of the disciples must give us pause. There is, of course, Simon Zelotes, i.e., Simon the Zealot, as modern translators render it. Granted, "the Zealot" might simply denote extraordinary piety, great religious zeal. But what might mark him out as exceptionally religious (i.e., fanatical) among a group of men who had abandoned home and family to follow a traveling guru, learning the arts of soapbox preaching and casting out demons? Wouldn't you say *all* these fellows qualified as "zealots"?

---

12. Eisler, pp. 265–267.

So what *else* might "the Zealot" have meant? During the Roman siege of Jerusalem a group of revolutionist *lestai* ("bandits") played a major role. While the group's name was a recent coinage, it represented the proud legacy of Judas the Galilean who had fomented the tax revolt against Rome in 6 C.E. They were in effect a new Hasmonean dynasty of freedom fighters. And, who knows? Perhaps the Zealot tag went back some years earlier. Or maybe tradition merely tagged Simon retrospectively with the slightly later term for revolutionaries. The punch line: one of Jesus' inner circle may have been a freedom-fighter.

Maybe not just one! Judas is dubbed "Iscariot." What does that mean? There is a hand full of possibilities, but probably the most popular among scholars is that "Iscariot" represents another revolutionist label, the *Sicarii*, or "dagger men," assassins who would slither through the crowds surrounding Roman officials and wealthy Jewish collaborators, short-swords up their sleeves, stab the victim, then join in the shouting while they slipped away undiscovered. Judas, then, may well be portrayed as another Zealot, "Judas the Sicarius."

Simon Peter is at one point (Matt. 16:17) called "Simon Bar-Jona," but this was not a typical Jewish patronymic (an epithet identifying you as So-and-so's son). Perhaps it originally denoted something else. There was another militant sect in New Testament times called the *Barjonim*, which means "the Terrorists,"[13] "the Extremists," "the Outlaws."[14] Was Peter a member? If three of the twelve look like Zealots, it would hardly be a surprise if the rest were, too. And what does that imply about

13. Oscar Cullmann, *Jesus and the Revolutionaries*. Trans. Gareth Putnam (New York: Harper & Row, 1970), p. 63.

14. Eisler, pp. 252–253.

Jesus? You know, don't you?

The Slavonic Josephus depicts Jesus as the favorite of the oppressed who pleaded with him to lead them in revolt against Rome, reviving and continuing the work of the Baptizer. Would he accede to their wishes? The text bears Christian interpolations at this and other points, their presence betrayed by narrative discontinuities and sudden incoherence. In some manuscripts, Jesus declines their invitation (precisely as in John 6:15): "But he did not heed it." But other manuscript evidence has him reply, "He did not disdain us."[15] A text critic must ask, which is the more difficult reading? The one more likely to have been changed to the other? So as Eisler translated the Slavonic text, Jesus is depicted as a revolutionary leader who justified Pilate's placard inscription, "Jesus of Nazareth, the man who would be king."

One dare not minimize the significance of the notorious saying, ""Do not think that I have come to bring peace on earth; I have not come to bring peace, but a sword. (Matt. 10:34). Luke has softened the saying, seeking to avoid the obvious: "Do you think I have come to give peace on earth? No, I tell you, but rather division" (Luke 12:51). This cannot be an authentic saying of Jesus (assuming there *are* any!). We need to recognize the analogy with Matthew 5:17–19.

> Think not that I have come to abolish the law and the prophets; I have come not to abolish them but to fulfil them. *For truly, I say to you, till heaven and earth pass away, not an iota, not a dot, will pass from the law until all is accomplished.* Whoever then relaxes one of the least of these commandments and

15. Eisler, p. 384 and note 18.

> teaches men so, shall be called least in the kingdom of heaven; but he who does them and teaches them shall be called great in the kingdom of heaven.

The italicized sentence, shared with Luke 16:15, appears already to be an anti-Marcionite saying. But Matthew has reinforced its point, fortifying it with the rest of the text: abolishing the Law and the Prophets is to abrogate the Hebrew scriptures *in toto*. Of course, this was the teaching of Marcion, and he took it to be the message of Jesus. As Bultmann[16] noted, when a gospel saying is introduced with "I came to" or "The Son of Man came to," the retrospective viewpoint signals that we are reading some Christian's attempt to sum up what he thinks Jesus was all about. In this case, the assertion is that Jesus' mission was to abolish the scriptures. In other words, that Jesus came to negate the Old Testament was a Christian belief, a belief held by one particular Christian faction. "Do not listen to those (Christian heretics) who spread such doctrines!" So here Jesus is (fictively) invoked as part of an anti-Marcionite polemic. What may we infer as to the *Sitz-im-Leben* (originary context) of the Matthean original of the "not peace but a sword" logion? I think it is obvious that what we have here is a Christian-Zealot rejection of the pacifistic self-makeover of the post-Jesus Christians. Christian pacifism is being rejected in the name of Jesus by those who wanted to carry on his revolutionary program.

For what it may be worth, Eisler, without laying great stress on it, notes that the third-century Roman official and persecutor of Christians under Diocletian, one Sossius, claimed that Jesus

---

16. Rudolf Bultmann, *The History of the Synoptic Tradition*. Trans. John Marsh (New York: Harper & Row, 1963), pp. 155–156.

was apprehended by the Jewish authorities after leading a band of some nine hundred men in a series of highway robberies. That would at least make some sense of John's account of Gethsemane where a full thousand soldiers (a cohort commanded by a *chiliarch*) were sent to capture Jesus.

Similarly, the *Toledoth Jeschu* depicts Jesus as leading a band of "hotheads" or radicals who fought on his behalf. This cannot be easily dismissed, since, as Hugh J. Schonfield pointed out, the *Toledoth Jeschu*, despite its reputation as a bitter Jewish parody of the Christian gospels, does not in fact caricature or malign Jesus. Instead, it quotes him repeatedly as citing this and that Old Testament text as a prophecy he, as the Messiah, has fulfilled—and no one even attempts to refute him! This tendency is so pronounced that Schonfield suggested that only a slight redactional spin has been applied to a Jewish-Christian gospel.[17] It would be very different if Jesus was consistently burlesqued throughout the document; then it would be quite natural to dismiss the portrayal of Jesus as mere polemical vilification. But it is not so.

Let's Go, Brandon!

An even stronger version of this "Zealot hypothesis" was set forth by S.G.F. Brandon in a pair of books, *The Fall of Jerusalem and the Christian Church* (1951)[18] and *Jesus and the Zealots*

---

17. Hugh J. Schonfield, *According to the Hebrews* (London: Duckworth, 1937).

18. S.G.F. Brandon, *The Fall of Jerusalem and the Christian Church* (London: SPCK, 1951).

(1967).[19] Zeroing in on a number of puzzling features of the gospel texts, Brandon said they make the most natural sense as loose ends that escaped the attention of the gospel writers as they sought to rewrite the history of Jesus.[20] Let's take a brief look at some of the main ones.

As for the incompletely erased remnants of the original, revolutionary Christianity, they are both minor and major. What did Jesus mean in Luke 22:36–37, "Let him who has no sword sell his cloak and buy one"? I'm guessing that the evangelist means to portray Jesus as setting the stage for the upcoming scene in the Garden of Gethsemane, where the disciples are to mount a token resistance to his arrest just so Isaiah 53:12 can be checked off the prophetic "To Do" list. Such a contrivance is fiction, not history. It is like Jim Phelps setting up some scam on *Mission Impossible.* Why cook up such nonsense? To substitute for an original account in which Jesus told them to arm themselves in order to fend off an anticipated ambush, which is of course exactly what happens in the Gethsemane scene. Only originally they weren't just kidding around. Brandon makes much of an implicit scenario of which most readers, laity and scholars alike, seem to remain oblivious, namely

> all the Evangelists agree on three essential points, namely that

---

19. S.G.F. Brandon, *Jesus and the Zealots: A Study of the Political Factor in Primitive Christianity* (New York: Scribners, 1967). I am leaving out of consideration Reza Aslan's sorry book, *Zealot: The Life and Times of Jesus of Nazareth* (New York: Random House, 2013), as it is completely derivative of Brandon but gives him virtually no acknowledgement.

20. Reimarus: "[T]he evangelists, in their history of Jesus, left unintentionally and through sheer carelessness, a few remaining traces of the reasons which influenced them at first in attributing to their master the object of becoming a worldly deliverer of Israel." P. 135.

> the disciples in Gethsemane were armed, that the Roman or Jewish officials sent to effect the arrest were heavily armed, obviously in anticipation of violent resistance, and that armed resistance was offered by the disciples.[21]

And in Luke 22:35–38, "Jesus took the precaution of seeing that his disciples were armed before going to Jerusalem."[22] Indeed,

> The fact that some, at least, of the disciples of Jesus were accustomed to go about with concealed weapons, after the manner of the Sicarii, is attested by Luke xxii.38. . . . If some of the disciples were accustomed to bear arms, and if Jesus on a critical occasion ensured that they were armed, the idea that the primitive Christian movement was pacific cannot be sustained.[23]

Conservatives and pacifists just cannot abide the literal meaning here. It gives them terrible theological indigestion. So they invoke what I like to call "the Irony Dodge."[24]

> Literally, but ironically—the words being spoken by Jesus in what Dr. Burkitt calls a mood of 'ironical foreboding'. The words "it is enough" might then be taken as a semi-playful rejoinder to the literally-minded disciples. The absurdly inadequate "two swords" are "enough" with which to resist the

---

21. Brandon, *The Fall of Jerusalem and the Christian Church*, p. 103.

22. Brandon, *Jesus and the Zealots*, p. 16.

23. Brandon, *Jesus and the Zealots*, p. 203.

24. Once at a meeting of the Jesus Seminar I proposed we add a fifth color bead. (We voted by dropping them into a basket.) Red meant Jesus certainly did or said it. Pink meant "probably authentic, with room for doubt." Gray denoted "unlikely but possible," while black meant "Forget it." My suggestion: purple, meaning Jesus *did* say it, but he was only kidding.

> might of Rome! So far being a summons to armed defence, Jesus' words are rather a wistful reminder of the utter futility of armed resistance.[25]

John's gospel seems to know there was a real battle in Gethsemane but sought to cover it up. He has a *chiliarchos*, captain of a *thousand* men, in charge of the operation, which would seem to imply a much bigger conflict than our Sunday School illustrations depict. But what happens to them? When Jesus identifies himself (or, as some think, utters the Divine Name, implying his use of magic, as he does in the *Toledoth Jeschu*), the soldiers scatter like bowling pins. This plainly did not happen, but it transparently veils what *did*: a battle issuing in a victory by Jesus and his men. Ah, if only!

Preparing for Battle

Gűnter Lűling, a student of Joachim Jeremias, was, like Julius Wellhausen, also an expert on ancient Arabian culture. As such, he was able to shed hitherto-unexpected light on aspects of the gospel portrayal of Jesus and the original facts possibly underlying them. One of his suggestions concerned the much-theorized saying of Jesus at table at the Last Supper, just before his ambush and arrest in Gethsemane. Lűling makes much of the Galilean identity of the Nazarene Jesus. He might, Lűling suggests, even be considered a Samaritan. In either case, what sort of a Messiah must he have considered himself? Not the Scion of the House

25. G.H.C. MacGregor, *The New Testament Basis of Pacifism* (New York: Fellowship of Reconciliation, 1936), p. 29.

of David, that's for sure, given the bitter resentments harbored generation after generation between the northern and southern Hebrew nations. Jesus is made the son of a man named Joseph in both Matthean and Lukan genealogies, and, though both try to connect Jesus, many generations back, to King David (a la Jewish/Judean expectation), this represents a Judaization of an original Jesus as "Messiah ben Joseph," heir to the throne of the Genesis Patriarch Joseph, progenitor of the tribes of Ephraim and Manasseh. And the role of this Ephraimite Messiah was to join battle with the heathen and to perish gloriously in combat. His redemptive death would absolve his people of their sins, clearing the way for divine intervention on Israel's behalf.

This is the deadly conflict for which, Lűling says, Jesus was preparing himself and his men in that Upper Room. And in this context, the words of Jesus, "He who has dipped his hand in the dish with me, will betray me" (Matt. 26:28) are not to be read as Jesus giving a secret signal to identify his betrayer, but rather a reflection of an ancient formula whereby conspirators in a vendetta, about to enact vengeance on an enemy (or enemies) swore, as a group, to die in the attempt if necessary. The scene did not envision various hands in turn dipping scraps of bread into herb sauce, but rather the hands of all present plunging into a common bowl containing the bloody, severed members of a sacrificial carcass, as an oath of commitment.

> It is readily apparent that the Galilean/Samaritan Jesus and his associates quite consciously celebrated, not the Passover procedures stipulated by the edicts of the priests, but rather those native to the context of the primeval Semitic society, built upon tribal structure, feuds and vendettas, and which in the context of Passover originally required the ritual of ham-

stringing (= hobbling, crippling by cutting the bull's hind leg tendons). The omission of the hobbling could be made up by the symbolically equivalent custom of not breaking the victim's bones.

The fashion in which the rite of Passover proceeded in ancient tribal society can hardly be reconstructed from the records drawn together much later under the auspices of the Jerusalem priesthood, for all the texts that would inform us of ancient practices against which both the state and its priesthood fought were expunged from the Old Testament. Nevertheless, a few scattered bits of text referring back to the archaic hobbling and dismemberment sacrifices do in fact exist. [. . .]

Presuming that the matter of "dipping hands in common in the bowl," was an insignificant detail, a fitful arabesque quite beside the main point, it wasn't fully expurgated from the gospel while, concurrently, it has never been given close attention in historically oriented, critical theology. The seemingly insignificant matter, however, that led to it never having been totally excluded from the gospels, provides us with substantial arguments emphasizing the martial character of Jesus' undertaking: If Jesus and his twelve disciples swore themselves mutually even unto death in the context of this ancient Semitic/ancient Israelitish—and anti-Jewish (!)—rite (and there is no way to get around this conclusion!), then logic compels us to accept that not only the disciples, but *Jesus* as well *was prepared* to take up arms and fight *to kill* to protect, as an example, one of his wounded fellows.[26]

---

26. Gűnter Lűling, "The Last Passover of Jesus and its Reinterpretation." Trans. Michael Conley. *Journal of Higher Criticism.* Vol. 12, no. 1, Spring 2006, pp. 95, 99.

Mark 14:20 has Jesus say, "It is one of the twelve, who is dipping bread in the same dish with me." What exactly is supposed to be going on here? Of course, we are told it is a Passover meal, implicitly involving the sharing of an animal sacrifice. Lűling emphasizes the fact that Jesus and his men are Galileans, heirs to a set of alternative Passover observances (some of which were echoed at Qumran). This opens the door to the possibility that the Last Supper connects with other pre-Deuteronomic northern Israelite customs as well, including one that might account for other elements of the Last Supper episode, namely a sacrificial ritual binding the participants in a planned vendetta. Those involved would pledge their loyalty to their comrades (fellow conspirators) even unto death ("'If I must die with you, I will not deny you.' And they all said the same" (Mark 14:31).

Swearing such an oath over a butchered sacrifice reflects both Judges 19: 29 ("And when he entered his house, he took a knife, and laying hold of his concubine he divided her, limb by limb, into twelve pieces, and sent her throughout all the territory of Israel.") and 1 Samuel 11:7 ("He took a yoke of oxen, and cut them in pieces and sent them throughout all the territory of Israel by the hand of messengers, saying, "Whoever does not come out after Saul and Samuel, so shall it be done to his oxen!" Then the dread of the Lord fell upon the people, and they came out as one man."). In both, the butchering and "sharing" of a corpse initiates vendetta with the implied threat of death. Then, as Lűling explains, the pledging ritual culminated in all the conspirators simultaneously dipping their right hands into a common bowl to bind themselves in sacred solidarity, even to the death.

This, Lűling maintains, was what Jesus and the twelve were really doing, preparatory to the planned conflict with the Romans, which did in fact erupt, albeit abortively, in Gethsemane soon afterward.

> This autonomy, verily, to one's death, manifested itself symbolically in the primeval, popular cutting of tendons and the dismembering of sacrifices as rites of covenant and the oaths of brotherly unanimity. The extent to which the secular/priestly central authority feared these plotters' rites is explicit in the fact that the rite of the "simultaneous-dipping-of-hands-in-the-dish" was verily persecuted inquisitorially: we learn from the Talmud that it was rigorously prescribed in the priestly supervised Passover that those partaking in the meal might not, under any circumstance, eat from a common bowl, but that each was to have his own separate dish - and that has remained the rule up to this very day. We do not know with absolute certainty whether this prohibition was in force in Jesus' day although this is extremely likely. But in any case, this information regarding the Talmud prohibition of eating from a common bowl, does permit us to conclude that the discrepancies in the four gospels reveal, full well, that the gospel writers were aware of the different meanings of eating from (a) one common bowl or (b) several separate bowls. The earliest of the gospels, Mark, provides the most clear-cut and briefest statement (14:20): "He answered and said unto them, 'It is one of the twelve that dippeth with me in the dish" [i.e. who will betray me]. This statement of Jesus means that one of those who took part in the Passover meal with him and the others and swore allegiance in the most primeval and solemn fashion, even at the cost of his life, will break his holy oath. In a certain sense this scene is consistent with Jesus' words to Peter, "Verily I say unto thee that this night, before the cock crow, thou shalt deny me thrice." (Matthew 26:34 and comparable passages in Luke and John). Here and in the other statements, the gravity of the betrayal is pointed out. The preposterous

thought, that the subsequent betrayer, Judas, precisely because he dipped into the bowl along with the others, may be the person to whom Jesus' words referred, is not present in this oldest version. In the light of what we know about the ancient Semitic rite of dipping one's hand in the bowl, Mark is simply reporting on the common Passover-hobbling-oath-taking rite of antique Semitic/Arabian/ Old Israelite origins.[27]

The later Lukan gospel, which softens down its message in other respects as well, tells us (22:21): "But behold, the hand of him that betrayeth me is with me on the table." Here the thought of designating the betrayer is totally absent. But in the case of Luke, it is quite clear what he is about in avoiding the phrase of "dipping hands in the bowl" in his account of Jesus' communion with his twelve disciples, for Luke sought to suppress any suggestion of swearing an oath—to the death—in a society well acquainted with this practice. He did not want Jesus to appear as one who had sworn an oath to be fulfilled to the death. This alteration, among many other aberrations, belongs to the efforts of the editors of the New Testament to make Jesus and his followers, after the fact, appear as pacifists.[28]

If Jesus and his twelve disciples swore themselves mutually even unto death in the context of this ancient Semitic/ancient Israelitic—and anti-Jewish (!)—rite (and there is no way to get around this conclusion!), then logic compels us to accept that not only the disciples, but *Jesus* as well *was prepared* to take up arms and fight *to kill* to protect, as an example, one of his wounded fellows. Jesus celebrated communion after the fashion of the primeval tribal society from which he came.[29]

27. Lűling, "Last Passover of Jesus," p. 98.
28. Lűling, "Last Passover of Jesus," pp. 98–99
29. Lűling, "Last Passover of Jesus," p. 99.

Tempter or Templar?

The most striking piece of evidence for a now-hidden militant Jesus must be the so-called Cleansing of the Temple. Mark seems to want to depict the event as if Jesus had merely burst into a church basement rummage sale, upsetting some card tables piled with old Readers Digest books. Did he know (or did he want his readers to know) that the Court of the Gentiles, containing the livestock stalls and coin exchange tables, was actually *ten acres* in size? And Jesus is said to have seized control of the whole space, since he was able to prevent anyone carrying sacrificial vessels through the area (Mark 11:16). And how could he have done that unless he had brought a large contingent of armed men with him? Now the whole thing might be pure fiction; that's entirely possible. But if there was any factual basis to it, Mark has suppressed the scale and the stakes of the scene. Remember how Mark notes in passing that Barabbas was to be executed for his role in "the insurrection"? *What* insurrection? Why, the one Jesus had provoked in the Temple only brief hours before: "the gospel evidence seems to indicate that Jesus' action in the Temple coincided with an insurrection in the city, in which Zealots appear to have been involved."[30]

A hitherto neglected possibility makes the whole scenario even more disturbing to those with conventional religious sensibility. Mark 15:6–15 relates that Pilate offered the gathered crowd a choice between Jesus and an insurrectionist named Barabbas, willing to release either of them as a gesture of Roman clemency. Barabbas "had committed murder in the insurrection"

30. Brandon, *Jesus and the Zealots*, p. 339.

(verse 7). At this point Matthew, repeating the story from Mark, seems to have added a striking detail. Some Old Latin manuscripts call the murderer "Jesus Barabbas." This looks to represent the original reading of Matthew, subsequently replaced by the simple "Barabbas." The reasoning is easy to see: scribes thought it almost blasphemous for this thug to share the holy name of Jesus (though it was a common name). But what exactly does "Jesus Barabbas" mean? Well, just as "Bartimaeus" means "Son of Timaeus," "Barabbas" means "Son of Abbas." "Abbas" remains a common Semitic name even today (cf., "Mahmoud Abbas"), but it is also the word for "father."

Call me suspicious, but I cannot help wondering whether, originally, the rebel Jesus Barabbas was "our" Jesus, and that *he* had been arrested for killing a Temple police guard who tried to turn back the assault on the Temple! But post-revolutionary Christians split the original account's single "Jesus" into the innocent "Jesus called the Christ" on the one hand and "Jesus Barabbas" on the other. The result, likewise distasteful to still later Christians, was a docetic "Jesus escapes crucifixion" story in which the "Jesus" who was let go was the Christian Savior, the Son of the Father, while "Jesus *called* Christ" (i.e., "falsely thought" to be the Savior) went to the cross in his place. But, on my theory, this is all part of the post-revolutionary Jesus Movement's retrospective whitewashing of their militant messiah, who got what the Romans thought he deserved. And of course this means that the Last Supper originally was set immediately *before* the Cleansing of the Temple, and that Jesus was arrested there on the spot.

Narnian Messiah

The latest advocate of a Zealot Jesus is Reza Aslan[31] (once, like Abdul Alhazred, an indifferent Muslim, then a born-again Christian convert, then a re-convert to Islam). I should imagine Aslan is taking a bit of a risk in publishing the work since his Jesus by no means conforms to Islamic Christology. He certainly rejects the Koranic doctrine of the virgin birth of Jesus and, even more important, the notion that Jesus escaped crucifixion, being caught up to heaven, with someone else crucified in his place. One might speculate that, by tying Jesus in with the revolutionary Zealots of first-century Palestine, he is constructing a Jesus in the image of Palestinian insurgents and Jihadis, but the fact that his Jesus remains a Jew makes that rather improbable. Besides, it remains a bit unclear whether Aslan actually thinks Jesus *was* a violent revolutionist. At first he seems to side with mainstream scholars like Hyam Maccoby, Richard A. Horsley, and John Dominic Crossan in understanding Jesus as more of a radical community organizer whose anti-Roman preachments, while not inciting violence, were deemed fatally dangerous by the Roman authorities.[32]

Aslan appears to be reinventing the chariot wheel. As we have seen, the case for Jesus as a Zealot-style revolutionary was set forth in a much stronger way decades ago by Robert Eisler and S.G.F. Brandon in *Jesus and the Zealots*. Aslan never refers to

---

31. Reza Aslan, *Zealot: The Life and Times of Jesus of Nazareth* (New York: Random House, 2013).

32. This is the problem with Peter Creswell's misleadingly titled *Jesus the Terrorist* (Washington: O Books, 2010). It turns out his view is much like those of Hyam Maccoby, John Dominic Crossan, and Richard A. Horsley: Jesus was a non-violent social radical.

Eisler, and he mentions Brandon only in a note and connected with a minor point. It may be a case of "the anxiety of influence," but it remains astounding that Aslan can either be ignorant of the work of these two titans or choose to ignore them, leaving the impression that his book possesses any novelty whatsoever. He is not the only contemporary scholar to behave this way, but one can only regret it.

Dr. Aslan is certainly a well-read scholar, despite his neglect of Eisler and Brandon, though I think his choice of Roman Catholic John Meier, whom I consider half an apologist, for a mentor is unfortunate. He is, all across the board, too optimistic about the accuracy of the gospel material. Like so many supposedly critical Jesus scholars, Aslan has not learned the lesson from William Wrede[33] that Mark is already dependent upon a complex reconstruction and by no means offers some primitive collection of authentic traditions as Aslan, like the Protestant liberals of old, imagines. Aslan knows Wrede but erroneously dismisses his theory by appeal to the crude, nonliterary Greek in which Mark's gospel is composed. Wrede did not think Mark the originator of the artificial secrecy motif but only the half-understanding inheritor of it. Besides, Mark is far from unsophisticated as a writer, as a reading of Robert M. Fowler's *Let the Reader Understand: Reader-Response Criticism and the Gospel of Mark*[34] will demonstrate. As a result, Aslan believes the Messianic secret was Jesus' own idea, a gross improbability in my view.

Aslan's case is founded on sand because of the numerous

---

33. William Wrede, *The Messianic Secret.* Trans. J.C.G. Greig. Library of Theological Translations (1901, rpt. Greenwood: Attic Press, 1971).

34. Robert M. Fowler, *Let the Reader Understand: Reader-Response Criticism and the Gospel of Mark* (Mineapolis: Fortress Press, 1901).

gospel passages he considers authentic Jesus sayings. The Lukan Woes (in his Sermon on the Plain, Luke chapter 6) do make Jesus sound like a rabble-rouser, but they appear to have been added by Luke himself as counterpoints to the Beatitudes he shares with Matthew, both deriving them from the Q Source. The Woes are not from Q.

Aslan discusses the Beelzebul Controversy, claiming the punchline ("If I cast out demons by the finger of God, then the kingdom of God has come upon you.") as a crucial piece of evidence that Jesus saw his exorcisms as the sign of the imminent manifestation of God's overthrow of Rome. But surely the saying, along with the whole story, is a Christian rewrite of the Exodus story in which Moses bests the Egyptian sorcerers in a miracle contest, whereupon his opponents admit that "this is the finger of God." It does not go back to Jesus, if there was a Jesus.

The Parable of the Good Samaritan, one of the favorites of the Jesus Seminar, must be a Lukan composition, but Aslan takes it as evidence of anti-clerical venom on Jesus' part, which would fit the anti-priestly sentiment of the Jews who put the priests to the sword and stopped the temple sacrifices offered on behalf of the emperor, the act which ignited the war with Rome. It would indeed, but it doesn't go back to Jesus.

Another uniquely Lukan passage that Aslan needs has Jesus asserting that "The kingdom of God is not coming with signs to be observed, . . . for behold: the kingdom of God is in your midst" (Luke 17:20–21). The problem this time is that the Greek word enteV usually means "within," not "in the midst of." The latter gained favor during a period in which "realized eschatology" was in vogue. Scholars of this persuasion preferred to picture Jesus proclaiming a kingdom already inaugurated invisibly in advance of its imminent eschatological denouement. They didn't like the traditional "within you" reading because that tended to fit a more abstractly ideal notion of the kingdom as an inner spiritual reality. But the text remains much more equivocal than Aslan wants it to be.

Aslan rests much weight on the famous "Render unto Caesar" passage understood in what strikes me as a very contrived manner. He imagines that by "Render unto Caesar that which is Caesar's and render unto God that which is God's," Jesus meant to say that faithful Jews need not hesitate to pay Roman taxes, since Caesar had minted them and might as well receive them back, idolatrous images and all, but that Jews ought to render the Holy Land back to God, its true owner, and expel the Roman occupiers. That seems to be blatant text twisting. On Aslan's own reading, the question "Is it lawful [for Jews] to pay taxes to Caesar?" only comes up as a trap. His enemies want to catch Jesus in treason, rejecting Jewish payment of Roman taxes. On Aslan's reading, Jesus walked right into their trap, gave them exactly what they wanted, and nothing happened. It seems clear to me that the point was to deny there was any compromise involved since Jews could not use Roman coins, with their images, to buy temple sacrifices anyway, so giving them to Rome represented no lapse in one's loyalty to God. You couldn't render Caesar's money to God.

It would come in handy if Jesus had been a carpenter, since Aslan could then paint him as a struggling peasant artisan. But the sole basis for this is Mark 6:3, "Is not this the carpenter," etc. But Geza Vermes[35] showed that "carpenter" in such a context

35. Geza Vermes, *Jesus the Jew: A Historian's Reading of the Gospels* (Lon-

(Jesus is expositing scripture in the synagogue) was a metaphor for a capable exegete of scripture.

Aslan really goes out on a limb when it comes to messianic titles. He concludes, after something of a tortuous argument, that "Son of Man," though (a la Vermes[36] and Maurice Casey[37]) never previously used as a messianic title, was made into one by Jesus himself in order to denote, albeit secretly, his messianic identity. In the nature of the case, it is very difficult to suppose that an ancient figure had in mind a secret meaning. If it was a secret, how can there be any real evidence for it? It looks more like a clever idea that a modern reader could not pass up.

Aslan also tells us, on the basis of John 4:25, that the Samaritan Taheb was synonymous with the Jewish Messiah. Surely that is an error on Aslan's part, based on a prior error by the Fourth Evangelist. The Messiah was to be a Davidic heir to the throne of Judah. Samaritans had centuries ago repudiated any and all ties to the Davidic monarchy of Judah and Jerusalem, and thus were in no hurry to see a new Davidic king arise. Instead, they hoped for the advent of the Taheb ("Restorer"), the "Prophet like Moses" to come and explain the problems of the Torah.

Aslan makes much of the difference between Jesus' confession before the Sanhedrin ("You will see the Son of Man sitting at the right hand of power and coming with the clouds of heaven," Mark 14:62; Matthew 26:64) and Stephen's vision in which "I see the Son Man standing at the right hand of God" (Acts

---

don: Fontana/Collins, 1976), pp. 21–22.

36. Vermes, *Jesus the Jew*, pp. 160–185.

37. Maurice Casey, *The Son of Man: The Interpretation and Influence of Daniel 7* (London: SPCK, 1979).

7:56). The former, Aslan says, denotes merely the enthronement of the Davidic king, which he supposes Jesus thought himself to be, while the latter envisions a god enthroned beside his divine father. But wait a second. Both passages have the enthronement at the right hand. What's the difference? How does one denote divinity, the other only royalty? Aslan says the pivot point was the change from Mark's "right hand of power" to Stephen's "right hand of God." Incredibly, Aslan accepts Thomas Aquinas's exegesis of "right hand of God" to mean "sharing the divine nature," whereas "right hand of power" just means Jesus sits in the catbird seat, period. This is absurd. Who does not know that "Power" used in such a context is simply a pious circumlocution for "God"? As many Jews do today, it was already customary to hallow the divine name by using a substitute term, as Hasidim today speak of God as "Hashem," the Name. In Mark 14:62, the High Priest does the same when he asks if Jesus believes himself to be "the son of the Blessed." By "the Blessed" he means "God."

He thinks the confusion between the supposedly different titles resulted from Stephen being an uneducated lout not versed in the Jewish scriptures. So the divinity of Christ arose from some dolt's insecure grasp of scripture that, uh—caught on? Not only is this just silly, but as soon as he blames a historical Stephen who said this very thing on a particular occasion, he shifts ground and admits that the whole speech of Stephen is a Lukan creation and not a record of a speech at all.

Maybe Reza Aslan should go back to the madrasa.

2 Whitewashing Empty Tombs

Brandon agreed with Eisler that, after the defeat and death of Jesus, his movement survived by the expedient of remaking itself, self-transforming into a kingdom not of this world but of the next. One might call the maneuver a retreat to either deferred eschatology or realized eschatology, or a synthesis of both. Albert Schweitzer[1] and his student Martin Werner[2] envisioned much the same process even though they believed Jesus was a quietist, awaiting the soon-coming End or perhaps hastening it by prompting a revival, a movement of national repentance, proving their worthiness for God at last to deliver them. In any case, it fizzled. Left holding the bag, Christians accommodated themselves to a continued existence in an unredeemed (or invisibly redeemed) world. Social and personal morality lost

---

1. Albert Schweitzer, *The Mystery of the Kingdom of God: The Secret of Jesus' Messiahship and Passion*. Trans. Walter Lowrie (New York: Schocken Books, 1964); Schweitzer, *The Quest of the Historical Jesus: A Critical Study of its Progress from Reimarus to Wrede*. Trans. W. Montgomery (New York: Macmillan, 1961).

2. Martin Werner, *The Formation of Christian Dogma: A Historical Study of its Problems*. Trans. S.G.F. Brandon (Boston: Beacon Press, 1965).

its radical edge, typical of sectarian movements in their second generation, perforce reassimilating to the mundane world which they had lately hoped to escape.

Once fearless in the face of martyrdom since it was an immediate elevator to heaven (Phil. 1:21–23), Christians learned to view the prospect of heaven as an eventual retirement home, "Paradise Acres." At first happy to give away one's savings to the poor and hungry, since they would soon be stuffing themselves at the Marriage Supper of the Lamb, Christians wound up thinking the tithe was not a bad idea after all.

And there was one particular item of Public Relations that required immediate attention: Christianity's revolutionary past had to be whitewashed lest Rome think Christians were still anti-Roman subversives and renew their persecution.

Justin Martyr is often quoted as saying (or implying) that all Christians had embraced peaceful non-resistance. Oh, to be sure, in their former, unenlightened days they deemed war allowable, even desirable. He seems to mean that all individual Christians have experienced this change of mind and heart as part of their Christian conversion.

> We, who had been filled with war and mutual slaughter and every wickedness, have each one—all the world over—changed the instruments of war, the swords into ploughs and the spears into farming implements, and we cultivate piety, righteousness, love for men, faith (and) the hope which comes from the Father Himself through the Crucified One.[3]

3. Justin, *Dialogue with Trypho* 110 (729).

Yet I cannot help wondering if he is tacitly admitting that, though Jesus' movement was initially one of violent revolution, it has abandoned it for the way of peace. Who knows?

Finally, what about the saying attributed to Jesus to the effect that he would soon destroy Herod's temple and replace it, miraculously, in a mere three days? Such wild boasts seem to have been common among contemporary messianic pretenders. Theudas the Magician promised he would divide the Jordan as Joshua, his role model, had once done (Josh. chapter 3. Uh, nice try!). The unnamed Egyptian prophet (Simon Magus? Ben Stada?) promised his followers that he would cause the walls of sinful Jerusalem to collapse, just Joshua had done at Jericho (Josh. chapter 6). Again, *bupkis.* Had Jesus, too, over-promised? And had his braggadocio gotten him, too, in big trouble with the law?

The first thing to notice is that the saying was something of a hot potato, and as such we see it tossed about from one New Testament writer to another. Mark has Jesus say, "I will destroy this temple that is made with hands, and in three days I will build another, not made with hands" (Mark 14:58). This has a theological ring to it, given the business of the replacement structure not being the product of human builders, like the New Jerusalem (Rev. 21:10–22), itself something of a substitute temple. But Mark ignores that and simply wipes it away as perjury from false witnesses. He doesn't know what it means, so he just wishes Jesus hadn't said it in the first place (though he did retain a similar statement in 13:2).

Perhaps Matthew noticed the incongruity in Mark's version and decided to snip the qualifications "made with hands," "not made with hands," in order to make it sound more like a magic trick, less like a possibly meaningful apocalyptic prophecy. After all, Mark's version would make sense if taken as a prophetic oracle representing the direct utterance of God, as often in the Old Testament prophets. In that case, Jesus wouldn't have meant that he himself would perform the trick, but that the Almighty could, and would, do it with a snap of his fingers.

Luke resorted to "surgical exegesis." For him, Jesus is not even alleged to have said it. Instead, it is credited to the proto-martyr Stephen (Acts 6:13–14), though it is still called a false testimony. "This Jesus of Nazareth will destroy this place, and will change the customs Moses delivered to us." How is Jesus, ostensibly a dead man, supposed to lay waste to the temple? If it ended right there, the accusation would make sense if they were saying Jesus had risen from the dead and would see to demolishing Herod's temple upon his soon return. But the saying continues: Jesus will supposedly abrogate the Torah of Moses, as later we will hear it alleged that Paul is doing that very thing already in this age (Acts 21:21). Even more confusing, does the "false" witness actually misrepresent Stephen's views? In the extemporaneous sermon he delivers to the lynch mob, Stephen in fact does at least intimate that building Solomon's temple was a mistake from the start. Why *wouldn't* God take a wrecking ball to it (or, by extension, Herod's)?

John admits Jesus did say, "Destroy this temple and in three days I will raise it [back] up" (John 2:19), but he makes it a metaphor for his own coming death and resurrection. Typically, his critics don't grasp his meaning.

Thomas has his own version: "I will destroy this house, and none shall be able to build it again." Thomas saying 71 provides no narrative context. My guess is that a Gnostic meaning is implied here: the esoteric teaching of Jesus, taken to heart, will put an end to one's weary round of reincarnation once and for all.

Such a variety of attempts to deal with this reported saying of Jesus implies they are all attempts to avoid its plain meaning, not to explicate it. It looks like the New Testament writers are protesting too much! Presumably, the evangelists would have passed over the saying in silence if they could, so the saying, picturing Jesus as a bomb-throwing anarchist, must have remained current for a long time, and, with it, the memory of Jesus as some kind of Zealot.

Revised Standard Version

I believe we may distinguish two subtly different approaches to de-fanging Christianity in the watchful eyes of Rome. The first is *revisionist history*. "It didn't happen like you've heard it did." As we have seen, both the Temple Cleansing and the Gethsemane confrontation appear to have been scaled down almost to insignificance in order to conceal the revolutionary character of both. But three more important texts require our attention. The first is Mark 12:35–37.

> And as Jesus taught in the temple, he said, "How can the scribes say that the Christ is the son of David? David himself, inspired by the Holy Spirit, declared,
>
> 'The Lord said to my Lord,
> Sit at my right hand,
> till I put thy enemies under thy feet.'
>
> David himself calls him Lord; so how is he his son?"

> Clearly Mark's purpose here is to refute a piece of teaching which he represents as coming from official Jewish sources. . . . The Messianic hope was known to be a potent factor in the development of extreme Jewish nationalism, and so the Markan repudiation of an interpretation of the Lord in terms of a decidedly Jewish nationalistic concept is easily understandable.[4]

That is pretty simple, it seems to me, especially when one compares it with the text-twisting attempts of conservative exegetes to make Jesus mean, e.g., that the Messiah (himself) was David's son but much more besides, i.e., God's Son. If we should ask why our own "scribes" say *that*, it's to rationalize the contradiction with their cherished Christology. The original assumption must have been to have Jesus reject Davidic/Judean messianism in favor of his being the Messiah of Ephraim, Messiah ben Joseph.[5]

Second, there is the series of verdicts and vindications of both Jesus and Paul, which, however, do not result in their being set free. Some justice system! Pilate declares Jesus innocent of all wrong-doing in Mark 15:14, Matthew 27:23–24, Luke 23:4, 14, 22, John 18:38; 19:4, 6. Herod Antipas clears him at Luke 23:14–15. The centurion at the foot of the cross exclaims, "Surely this man was innocent!" (Luke 23:47). One of the two rebels crucified alongside him mocks him, but the other defends Jesus' innocence (Luke 23:40–41). Paul is exonerated in Acts

4. Brandon, *The Fall of Jerusalem and the Christian Church*, pp. 189, 191.

5. David C. Mitchell, *Messiah ben Joseph* (Newton Mearns, Scotland: Campbell Publications, 2021).

16:35–40; 18:12–17; 19:40–41; 22:25; 23:9, 29; 25:10, 18, 25; 26:31–32; 28:18, 21. It is possible that the New Testament narrators have accurately related the legal misadventures of their heroes, but one can well imagine readers who harbored suspicions against the leaders of the sect, asking themselves if there must have been something to the accusations after all. Could *all* these cases have been mere misunderstandings? But in any case, it is apparent that the Christian writers had their work cut out for them, striving to get their young and controversial movement out from a black cloud of suspicion.

Third, there is the tell-tale shifting of the blame for Jesus' death from the Romans to the Jews. In broad outline, the story of Jesus' arrest, condemnation, and execution tends toward the conclusion that the Roman occupiers believed that Jesus and his movement posed a potential but real threat to Roman authority. Probably no Romans feared that Jesus and his "troops" could actually expel the Roman eagle, but there was sufficient reason to believe an unnecessary bloodbath might be in the offing—unless they nipped it in the bud. This must have become perfectly clear in the wake of the Temple Cleansing spectacle. If Jesus's men could commandeer the Court of the Gentiles, they might be able to despoil the temple treasury, too, and arm themselves. So Jesus gets arrested after an armed scuffle of unknown proportions, then interrogated by Pilate, and finally crucified, the penalty reserved for thieves, runaway slaves—and seditionists. What other ingredients would have been required?

But of course, additional flesh has been larded on these bones. Jewish flesh. As we now read the canonical gospels, it is not the Roman authorities but their Jewish counterparts who first recognize the threat Jesus poses for Rome. In John 11:45–

53, we eavesdrop on a meeting of the Jewish Sanhedrin. They are alarmed at the mounting popularity of Jesus and the growth in the ranks of his followers. "His half-witted fans will go out of control!"[6] If present trends continue, the Romans will not hesitate to put a stop to it, coming down hard not only on the Jesus sect but the Jewish nation as a whole. But Pontius Pilate and his administration appear oblivious of the danger; hence it falls to the Sanhedrin to give them a push, which they go on to do. Now our suspicions are already aroused: why would the Roman occupiers be asleep at the switch? Pilate had swatted lesser flies than Jesus before! Thus the role of the Sanhedrin looks artificial and forced. And the ineptitude of the Romans appears equally artificial, which of course it is. The facts are being tendentially fictionalized to get Rome (whom Mark desires to conciliate) off the hook.

We have a pretty clear idea of what sort of person Pontius Pilate was. His anti-Semitic outrages are amply recorded by both Philo and Josephus. It would be expected that, when briefed about Jesus and his recent arrest, he would not have long deliberated. Yet the gospels depict him as exceedingly reluctant to condemn Jesus. He cannot see why the Jews are persecuting the poor fellow; maybe they're just jealous of his popularity (Matt. 27:18). In other words, there could have been no real fault in Jesus, no good reason to condemn him.

The evangelists are conspicuously aware that their portrayal of Pilate as trying to set Jesus free is implausible, given what the reader must know of Pilate's reputation, so they introduce contrived reasons for his merciful mood: Pilate's wife threw a

---

6. Tim Rice, *Jesus Christ Superstar* (Deca Records, 1970).

scare into him by passing him a note about a premonitory dream she had about Jesus. For *our* sake, not his, give the guy a break (Matt. 27:19)!

But, in the end, Pilate behaves with uncharacteristic clemency because the mob gathered outside his window threaten to rat him out to Rome (John 19:12). Pilate? Bullied by a bunch of nameless roustabouts? It's not like he's afraid of losing their votes! My guess is that this part of the story is based on a real incident featuring Pilate: when someone claiming to be the Samaritan Prophet Like Moses gathered a crowd at Mount Gerizim, Pilate sent troops to disperse them with a little help from their swords. It was a massacre, and surviving Samaritans reported Pilate's cruelty to the home office. The procurator was recalled to Rome for thus making a mockery of Roman justice (Josephus, *Antiquities of the Jews* 18.4.1–2). Pilate had gone too far but was no doubt taken aback at receiving his pink slip. The gospel writers, I suggest, knew of this incident and, in effect, retrojected it into the case of Jesus, as if Pilate was already aware of the possible repercussions of dealing harshly with a messianic pretender. But it's fiction.

And Barabbas! We are supposed to believe that Pilate would set free one prisoner as a gesture of good will at Passover time. His two finalists are Jesus and the insurrectionist Barabbas. Pilate asks for a show of hands, evading blame by handing the decision over to this bunch of half-drunk idlers: Who do you want, the innocent Jesus or the convicted murderer Barabbas? Remember, Barabbas was a captured terrorist! The mob bullies Pilate into setting Barabbas free, lest Caesar should hear of it and fire Pilate. But wouldn't Pilate be more afraid of Caesar's displeasure if he released this PLO fighter? It is absurd. Why was the story fabricated? Christians knew they could not get away with simply denying that Jesus died by Roman decree, but they did their best to exonerate Pilate anyway. This tendency went so far that eventually Pilate was canonized as a saint in the Coptic Church!

So Jews are blamed for engineering the death of Jesus by manipulating the benevolent Roman cops on the beat. And we are not surprised to see the sequence of implausibilities and goofs that infest the story. First, to whom do we owe the account of the Sanhedrin trial? Who was there to take notes for the disciples? Were they eavesdropping at the window? Did they have the place bugged? Oh, but wasn't Joseph of Arimathea a secret follower of Jesus? He might have filled in Peter and the rest afterward, right? But Mark never says Joseph was a Jesus sympathizer nor gives any hint that he had voted to acquit: "And they all condemned him as deserving death" (Mark 14:64). It is only subsequent gospels in which Joseph receives added layers of sanctification. True, Mark has Joseph arrange a decent burial for Jesus, but this need not imply he had any special fondness for Jesus. Burial of the dead, especially when no one else would do it, was esteemed one of the chiefest works of virtue in Judaism, as witness the Book of Tobit.

What, pray tell, was the Sanhedrin doing meeting on Passover Eve, when they, of all people, must have been observing the seder in their homes? And what was the specific blasphemy Jesus was supposed to have committed during the interrogation? Claiming to be the Messiah? That was no blasphemy. Someone had to be the Messiah, and anyone might be! A century later, Simon bar Kochba came forward as King Messiah and, a la John the Baptist, Rabbi Akiba endorsed his claim. It turned out

Simon had jumped the gun, but neither Simon nor Akiba was considered a blasphemer or a heretic. Surely the gospels have included an anachronism, picturing later Jewish versus Christian debates over whether Jesus was a divine being or a second god.

Finally, as Conzelmann[7] noticed, this programmatic transfer of blame from Romans to Jews explains the otherwise puzzling transference of the mocking torment of the purple-clad, black-and-blue Jesus from Pilate's troops to those of Herod Antipas (cp Luke 23:11 and Mark 15:16–20).

Jesus Was Somebody Else

Lena Einhorn[8] puts our puzzle pieces together in a different and daring way. She contends that Jesus is the Talmudic character Ben Stada, just as most Talmudic authorities surmise. Both are said to have emerged from Egypt carrying magic sigils inscribed in their flesh. Jesus is also said in the *Toledoth Jeschu* to have hidden a paper note containing the magically potent Tetragammaton beneath a flap of his flesh. Others have theorized that Ben Stada is the Egyptian messiah mentioned by both Josephus (*Jewish War* 2:13.5; *Jewish Antiquities* 20:8:6) and Acts. According to Einhorn, both guesses are correct. Paul is *rightly* taken for him in Acts 21:38, because Paul was Jesus was the Egyptian was Ben Stada. Along the same lines, John

---

7. Hans Conzelmann, , *The Theology of St. Luke*. Trans. Geoffrey Buswell (New York: Harper & Row, 1961), p. 87.

8. Lena Einhorn, *The Jesus Mystery: Astonishing Clues to the True Identities of Jesus and Paul*. Lyons Press (Globe Pequot Press, 2007); Einhorn, *A Shift in Time: How Historical Documents Reveal the Surprising Truth about Jesus* (Yucca Publishing, 2016).

the Baptist was in realty the same man as Theudas the Magician. Both were linked to the Jordan, and both were beheaded by the authorities. In the gospels and Acts, the historical events have been retrojected to an earlier decade.

Why on earth would the gospel writers have done this? The answer is not terribly far to seek. As Einhorn points out, secular sources have it that nothing much out of the ordinary troubled Palestine in the 30s, a fact that ill befits the assumptions of Liberation Theology and all those who would make the historical Jesus a first-century Che Guevara. By contrast, the fifties were turbulent with revolutionary unrest. The hypothesized historical retrojection of Jesus from the fightin' fifties to the relatively pacific twenties, and especially fragmenting him into several different characters, would have the effect of, yet again, whitewashing the revolutionary Jesus, enemy of Rome, into a safely nonpartisan sage who was framed by his jealous rivals and crucified by Rome, even though Pilate had to be blackmailed to sentence him.

Einhorn opts for the Swoon Theory, noting that it is by no means ridiculous despite the uneasy assurances of apologists. She regards the real Jesus as a Zealot crucified alongside fellow Zealots ("thieves," *lestai*). After his escape from the cross, he went elsewhere preaching a new gospel concerning the true meaning of the resurrection he had just undergone. So the Proclaimer became the Proclaimed—as well as the Proclaimer of the Proclaimed!

Einhorn thus makes sense of the extensive parallels between the Passion journeys of both Jesus and Paul in Luke-Acts, not that it all happened twice, but that the second telling of the story in Paul's case is a hint that Paul is the same character who underwent the process in Luke. Einhorn notes other, smaller parallels including the Galilean birthplace of Paul according to Jerome and the similarity of Paul's being trained as a youth by Gamaliel and Jesus engaged in dialectic with the elders and scribes in the Temple at age 12. She suggests that Pilate's uncharacteristic urgency to have Jesus acquitted might be explained as another version of Acts 22:25–29, in which the Roman official, about to flog Paul, stands down when he discovers the object of his wrath is a Roman citizen. The Talmud says, cryptically, that Jesus, too, had some connection with the government.

This all may seem an extreme measure, but it would certainly account for some irresistibly suggestive notes in the gospels, such as Jesus' presence with a crowd of followers out in the wilderness, leading to his feeding miracles, in turn fueling the people's zeal to lift him onto their shoulders and carry him into Jerusalem as their new king (John 6:14–15). Think also of the warning in the Olivet Discourse where Jesus warns his disciples not to fall for conspiratorial urgings of "Behold! He is in the desert! Behold, he is waiting in the inner room!" (Matt. 24:26). It sounds like some Christians are in danger of jumping the apocalyptic gun to follow some phony like Theudas or the Egyptian.

Speaking of striking parallels between the Jesus story and those of other contemporary messianic leaders, what are we to make of the Cleansing of the Temple complex? When Jesus is hailed as king by the Palm Sunday crowds waving palm branches, can there be some sort of connection to the Temple authorities welcoming the forces of John of Gischala with olive branches (whether literally or figuratively hardly matters)? And why was John headed there? Why, to *clean out* the rival rebel faction (*lestai*, "robbers") of Simon bar Gioras.[9] In other words, he cleansed the Temple, because it had degenerated into a den of thieves.

Similarly, Plutarch relates the death of Cleomenes,[10] the revolutionary King of Sparta, having fled to Alexandria. As enemy guards close in on him, he leads his men in group suicide (a la Masada). When the guards arrive, they stab the bodies just to make sure they're dead (as in John 19:34). When pious women come to view his corpse displayed on a cross, they are amazed to see carrion birds protecting the rebel king's features, prompting them to declare him a son of the gods!

There are two ways to go with this. We might say, "The Jesus story is so like these others, we ought, by the principle of analogy, to conclude that the historical Jesus belongs among the ranks of such revolutionary radicals ("numbered among the transgressors," you might say). Or we might begin to wonder if instead what has happened is that many early Christians inadvertently conflated details of these various messiahs with the story of Jesus. In fact, isn't that perhaps what "Jesus" is retroactively warning Christians not to do in Mark 13:5–6, 21–23?[11]

---

9. Flavius Josephus, *The Jewish War*. V. IX. 11. G.A. Williamson Trans.

10. Plutarch's *Lives of the Noble Greeks and Romans*, "Cleomenes." Dryden Trans.

11. In fact, here I think of Reinhold Niebuhr's demythologization of biblical apocalyptic as limit language. In such warnings, Christians are not to calculate their expectations for the real Messiah, so as to be sure not to miss him when at last he arrives. Nay, rather the point is to accept the fact that all messianic forecasts and pretensions ought to be disregarded because they will never, in the real world, fail to disappoint. It is a warning against delusional fanaticism. See Reinhold Niebuhr, *The Nature and Destiny of Man: A Christian Interpretation* (New York: Scribners, 1948), Vol II, p. 178: "It is a good thing to seek for the Kingdom of God on earth; but it is very dubious to claim to have found it. In that claim some new relativity of history and some new egoistic force

Daniel T. Unterbrink adopts a similar approach in his book *Judas the Galilean: The Flesh and Blood Jesus.*[12] The title pretty much says it all; you start out knowing the butler did it. The verdict? The Jesus character of the gospels, strictly speaking, did not exist. But in another sense, he did, that is, if you can get used to calling him "Judas of Galilee." Now, he *did* exist, or so it seems if you employ your code-cracking skills to read between the lines of Josephus. Unterbrink cannot help noticing certain parallels between the militant founder of the Fourth Philosophy, the prototype for the slightly later Zealot movement, and the eponymous founder of Christianity. Call me reductionistic, but I think it all boils down to three similarities. First, both men were from places in Galilee. Second, both had a following of devoted disciples. Third, both were executed by the Romans for urging tax revolt. The rest of the *thirty* parallels Unterbrink offers us strike me as trivial and far-fetched (not that the three I listed don't).

His case is marred by several methodological flaws. For one thing, he seems inconsistent in his skepticism about the gospel accounts of the teaching of Jesus. When it suits him, he swallows as authentic logia Bultmann wouldn't touch with a ten-foot pole. Otherwise, Unterbrink is quite happy to dismiss an assertion in Acts or the gospels as tendentious distortions because their implications, if genuine, would work against his schema. For another, he places too much weight on highly debatable interpretations, e.g., that the crucial "Render unto Caesar" saying

---

make pretensions of sanctity which, at best, are merely absurd and, at worst, unleash new furies and fanaticisms."

12. Daniel T. Unterbrink, *Judas the Galilean: The Flesh and Blood Jesus* (New York: iUniverse, 2004).

really meant "Romans go home!"[13] Not infrequently, he seems to silently take for granted as fact tenuous interpretations and identifications suggested earlier in the argument. He commends his theory for its ability to make the most comprehensive sense of all the data: "Everything fits, unlike most other hypotheses about Jesus."[14] Maybe—if you strain out a gnat and swallow a camel. He forthrightly admits he is "trying to tie together Judas and Jesus."[15] But that's just the problem.

The argument of *Judas the Galilean* is at the same time based upon and vitiated by the tacit assumption that there were only a handful of people in ancient Judea, so if we run across the same name twice, both must refer to the same individual. All the various Simons must be the same guy. Ditto all the Judases, etc. Unterbrink is thus reducing, and therefore eliminating, a number of variables in order to simplify his equation.

Our author has learned another name game from Robert Eisenman,[16] who, alert to easily overlooked anomalies such as Mary the mother of Jesus having a sister named Mary[17] (John 19:25), proposed that such characters had been split up so as to separate the increasingly transcendent Jesus from any messy

---

13. See the scene from *Monty Python's "The Life of Brian (of Nazareth)"* in which a Roman officer nabs Brian in the act of painting "Romans Go Home" across a huge, white-washed wall and corrects his Latin. Graham Chapman, John Cleese, Terry Gilliam, Eric Idle, Terry Jones, and Michael Palin, *Monty Python's The Life of Brian (of Nazareth)* pp. 41–44.

14. Unterbrink, p. 156.

15. Unterbrink, p. 156.

16. Robert Eisenman, *James the Brother of Jesus: The Key to Unlocking the Secrets of Early Christianity and the Dead Sea Scrolls* (New York: Viking/Penguin, 1997).

17. Eisenman, *James the Brother of Jesus*, pp. 198–199, 478, 592, 597, 770–771, 778–779, 840.

physical connections to mere mortals. The same tendency motivates the Roman Catholic insistence that the "brothers" of Jesus (Mark 6:3) are instead "cousins." They *have* to be! Well, Unterbrink becomes the Sorcerer's Apprentice, recasting Mary as Jesus' *wife* (married at Cana) and James, Jude, Simon, and Joses as Jesus's own *sons*.[18] It's like a play with more roles than players, so that each actor must portray two characters.

Unterbrink exhibits the typical "village atheist" loathing for Paul, painting him as a pathological liar and charlatan who belonged in an insane asylum.[19] He sneers at Paul's claims to have learned about Jesus *from* Jesus in a series of dreams and trances.[20] Forgive me, but I cannot help applying the same criticism to Unterbrink's *Judas the Galilean*: it seems to be a fragile web of thinly, albeit intricately woven, surmise and speculation. But in any case, it counts as another contemporary version of the "Zealot Jesus" hypothesis.

Luigi Cascioli, in *The Fable of Christ: Book of Accusation*,[21] fields a somewhat similar theory, though technically it is a variety of Christ Mythicism. Cascioli, you may recall, brought suit against the Vatican for purposely hoodwinking its flock for many centuries. They knew good and well that their precious (and useful) Jesus, in whose holy name they had intimidated and exploited so many for so long, simply never existed in the first place. But *some*body did, and he was a Jewish, anti-Roman freedom fighter: John of Gamala, Judas of Galilee's number one

18. Unterbrink, pp. 104–107.

19. Unterbrink, p. 72.

20. Unterbrink, p. 72.

21. Luigi Casciololi, *The Fable of Christ: Book of Accusation* (np: Luigi Pascioli, 2001).

son. How did this come about? Cascioli pictures the Essenes as a militant sect who several times sought to put the Qumran War Scroll into action, though suffering a string of devastating defeats, being hopelessly outgunned by the hated Gentiles. They were led by Judas' five sons, one after the other. They knew God had led their forbears to victory over the persecuting Seleucids by the hand of the Hasmoneans, so why was he looking the other way at their attempts to kick out the Romans?

Hmmmm . . . what if God *had* sent the longed-for messianic leader, who, however, went unrecognized? Sure! *That* would explain it! All right, they were still stuck in This Fallen Age, but at least they didn't have to imagine God had forgotten them. But the new theory would never work if left as an abstract possibility, so they began to flesh out the concept, and they hit upon Judas the Galilean's son, John of Gamala, as their model. The result was not to identify John himself as the unrecognized Messiah, but rather to use him as a mannequin on which to hang the messianic robes. The gospel Jesus was the result. You might say he had not saved them as expected, but he had, in some measure, saved *face* for them. But this would count as another theory making "Jesus" a revolutionary.

Ralph Ellis,[22] in a series of astonishing works, raises (and answers) the question: given the ostensible history-shaking importance of Jesus Christ, why does he not come in for mention in any contemporary historical report? (The snippets left by both Josephus and Tacitus, even if genuine, are still late enough and cursory enough to be no more than second-hand echoes

---

22. Ralph Ellis, *Cleopatra to Christ: Jesus Was the Great Grandson of Cleopatra* (Cheshire: Edfu Books, 2017).

of Christian preaching.) Mythicists infer from this that there was no historical Jesus on whom to report. Mainstream scholars adopt the self-contradictory notion that the historical Jesus was a pretty unexceptional character who wouldn't merit mention by historians, which invites the question of how such a relative non-entity could have ignited a world religion. Ralph Ellis, by contrast, argues that Jesus not only deserved far-reaching notoriety but did in fact garner the appropriate coverage, albeit under many names, titles, and epithets. Among many others, he was known as Jesus of Gamala, one of the attested sons of Judas the Galilean, founder of the Fourth Philosophy. The others have equally famous names, Simon and James. Ellis also identifies the gospel Jesus with Jesus son of Sapphias, a revolutionary bandit, and the doom-saying prophet Jesus ben Ananias, all chronicled by Josephus. Jesus of Gamala headed up a powerful army, 600 strong, with considerable resources in an autonomous district (Bethanya, or Bethany) settled by Persian royalty in exile. Tolerated at first by Rome, they clashed over the taxation census that brought Judas the Galilean into revolt against Rome in 6 CE.

These are only some of the very many aliases of Jesus according to Ellis, but the rest are beyond the scope of our discussion. Lest the reader recoil, as many do, from such an unfamiliar account of Jesus, let me try to soften the blow, at least on one point. Keep in mind that the sharing of names between and among disparate individuals is not unexampled in the Bible. Is the disciple Thaddeus the same as Lebbaeus (as in some manuscripts)? Was he alternatively called Theudas or Addai, or Judas or "Judas not Iscariot"? Was Nathaniel also Bartholomew? Was Levi sometimes known as Matthew? How many Marys belonged to Jesus' entourage? Did Paul also go by "Saul"? Were

Paul and Simon Magus and Elymas, Etoimas, Atomus, and Bar-Jesus really the same man? How about Simon, Symeon, Simon of Cyrene, Simon Zelotes, Simon Magus, Simon the Pharisee, Simon the Leper, Simon the Tanner, Peter, and Cephas? Then there are James the Greater, James the Lesser, and James the Just (not to be confused with "Jesus Justus," please!).

And, yes, "Jesus," like the rest of these names, was quite common, but Ralph Ellis is not the only scholar[23] to identify Jesus Christ with Jesus ben Ananias, of whom Josephus recounts the following.

> But a further portent was even more alarming. Four years before the war, when the city was enjoying profound peace and prosperity, there came to the feast at which it is the custom of all Jews to erect tabernacles to God, one Jesus, son of Ananias, a rude peasant, who suddenly began to cry out, "A voice from the east, a voice from the west, a voice from the four winds, a voice against Jerusalem and the sanctuary, a voice against the bridegroom and the bride, a voice against all the people." Day and night he went about all the alleys with this cry on his lips. Some of the leading citizens, incensed at these ill-omened words, arrested the fellow and severely chastised him. But he, without a word on his own behalf or for the private ear of those who smote him, only continued his cries as before. Thereupon, the magistrates, supposing, as was indeed the case, that the man was under some supernatural impulse,

---

23. Theodore J. Weeden, "The Two Jesuses," *Foundations and Facets Forum* (New Series 6, 2, Fall 2003), demonstrates in detail how Josephus' account of Jesus ben Ananias must have been freely adapted as the Passion of Jesus in all four canonical gospels. This is not to say, as Ellis does, that Jesus Christ and Jesus ben Ananias were the same man, but rather that the story of the latter has been reassigned to the former, and this is not far from Ellis's methodology. See also Price, *Deconstructing Jesus*, pp. 243–244.

> brought him before the Roman governor; there, although flayed to the bone with scourges, he neither sued for mercy nor shed a tear, but, merely introducing the most mournful of variations into his utterances, responded to each lashing with "Woe to Jerusalem!" When Albinus, the governor, asked him who and whence he was and why he uttered these cries, he answered him never a word, but unceasingly reiterated his dirge over the city, until Albinus pronounced him a maniac and let him go. During the whole period up to the outbreak of war he neither approached nor was seen talking to any of the citizens, but daily, like a prayer that he had conned, repeated his lament, "Woe to Jerusalem!" He neither cursed any of those who beat him from day to day, nor blessed those who offered him food: to all men that melancholy presage was his one reply. His cries were loudest at the festivals. So for seven years and five months he continued his wail, his voice never flagging nor his strength exhausted, until in the siege, having seen his presage verified, he found his rest. For, while going his round and shouting in piercing tones from the wall, "Woe once more to the city and to the people and to the temple," as he added a last word, "and woe to me also," a stone hurled from the ballista struck and killed him on the spot. So with those ominous words still upon his lips he passed away. (Flavius Josephus, *The Wars of the Jews*. Book 6, Chapter 5, Section 3, Whiston Trans.)

Accommodation of Desolation

The second way in which the gospel material has been affected by the defeat of the revolutionary Jesus party[24] is simple accom-

---

24. Hugh J. Schonfield, *The Jesus Party* (New York: Macmillan, 1974).

modation or resignation to the facts of victorious Roman rule. Joseph Atwill[25] sums up the result.

> The only works to have survived this century of religious warfare, the Gospels and the histories of Josephus, had a pro-Roman perspective. In the case of Josephus' histories this is hardly surprising, as he was an adopted member of the imperial family. It is notable, however, that the New Testament also has a point of view positive to the Romans. The first century was not a time when one would expect that a Jewish cult with a viewpoint favorable to the Empire would have emerged. Yet the New Testament texts never portray Roman soldiers in a negative light,[26] and actually describe them as "devout" and God-fearing. [Acts 10:1–2] . . . The New Testament also presents tax-collectors, who would have been working for the Romans, in a favorable light. . . . The citizenship espoused in the works of Josephus and the New Testament would have been seen favorably by Rome. Each work proclaims the holiness of subservience. And each takes the position that, as it is God who has given the Romans their power, it is therefore against God's will to resist them.

Though these phenomena might be interpreted in various ways (see below), the implication need not be any more shocking than to observe that, after the failed Jewish Revolt, messianic Jewish Christians simply acquiesced to the new harsh realities by adopting the traditional stance of the pre-war Pharisees and Sadducees: "Yes, it is fine in theory to say that Jehovah is the only King of the Jewish nation, but this particular Goliath just

---

25. Joseph Atwill, *Caesar's Messiah: The Roman Invention of Jesus*. Flavian Signature edition (Charleston: CreateSpace, 2011), p. 27.

26. Well, maybe except for Mark 15:16–20!

doesn't seem likely to go down! Better get used to it, folks! Better red than dead! Maybe the Romans won't treat us so badly if we don't treat them like monsters."

I suggest this represents the understanding behind texts like Matthew 5:41: "If anyone forces you to go with him one mile, go with him two miles." The reference is to a law of the occupation whereby any road-weary Roman legionary could commandeer one of the native population to shoulder the soldier's field pack and join him for one mile on his journey. It is a kind of "work of supererogation," doing more than strictly commanded and at the same time "killing 'em with kindness." Why not? Does a Jew have to hate every Roman?

Similarly, the famous "render unto Caesar" anecdote avoids trouble by cleverly defusing the ticking bomb. Is it taking the mark of the Beast for a Jew to pay taxes to Rome? Is it really worth getting martyred to stand up for your principles? Jesus neatly solves the problem by pointing out that Caesar's profile stamped onto the denarius marks the coin as belonging to the Roman government. What compromise can be entailed if the law requires you to return his coins to him? Conversely, since they do carry a "graven image" they are idolatrous "filthy lucre" which must not be offered to God. After all, that's why there were money changers in the Jerusalem temple! So no problem! God gets one variety of currency; Rome gets another! That's not compromise; it's just coexistence.

One thinks here also of a pair of healing stories, possibly Q and Mark versions of a single original. Mark 7:24–30 tells of a Syro-Phoenician (i.e., Gentile) woman whose daughter, in no condition to travel, languishes back home in a makeshift straitjacket in the grip of demonic possession. She has somehow learned that Jesus is in town and finds him. She pleads for him to exorcize the girl, presumably hoping Jesus will make a house call. He tests her faith with a pose of indifference (rather like the priest and the Levite in the Good Samaritan story). But she refuses to give up. and Jesus dismisses her with the assurance that the demon has already vacated the premises as they stood there talking!

The twin of that healing story is found in Luke 7:1–10 and Matthew 8:5–13. Again, a Gentile, this time a Roman centurion, requests a healing from Jesus. In Matthew the man approaches Jesus in person, asking him to heal his child (or favorite slave, since the word *pais* could mean either). He says he knows Jesus can do it because he knows how authority works; as a military commander, he knows his orders will be carried out. He perceives that Jesus possesses such authority, no doubt because of his reputation. To the officer it seems merely logical, but Jesus acclaims his faith as greater than any he has encountered among his own nation! Jesus is more than willing to follow the centurion home to the sufferer's sickbed, but the centurion will not have it! He (as a Gentile) judges himself unworthy (because ritually unclean?) to have Jesus enter his home. All right, then; Jesus heals the lad at a distance! He also announces that the Gentile's faith, unparalleled for the present, will, at the banquet of salvation, be revealed to have been quite common, and in such numbers as to scandalize chauvinistic Jews. What might account for such an unexpected legion of Gentiles rubbing elbows with the Hebrew Patriarchs?

The Gentile Mission, of course! There was no gospel preaching venture in Jesus' own lifetime, and the gospel writers did not feel at liberty to introduce an anachronism to that effect. Some came close, as witness Matthew's Great Commission in which the Risen Christ (i.e., not the remembered historical Jesus) commands his disciples (who stand for Matthew's Jewish Christians in Antioch) to recruit Gentiles wherever they find them. Others were not quite so bold, being content merely to intimate such a missionary agenda. That is the point of both stories of Jesus healing at a distance. The symbolism is unmistakable. Jesus, prevailed upon to heal a sufferer, does so, but *at a great distance.* The sufferer is a Gentile and *a member of the next generation.* That is the post-Jesus Gentile Mission, and Jesus is active no longer in person but invisibly through the hands of his successors.

The Cornelius story of Acts chapters 10 and 11 can be read, without contrivance, as a nonviolent continuation of the long-standing tensions between Jewish nationalists, exalting the superior position of the Jewish people, and assimilationist, Hellenistic Jews eager to take their place among the family of nations. Peter starts out a nationalist, unwilling to recruit non-Jews to faith in Jesus (no doubt because God had a separate plan in mind for them).[27] But Peter winds up convinced despite himself that the message of Jesus is for all pious people of whatever nation. We can observe the same continuing stresses threatening to destroy Christian unity when we read the Epistle to the Galatians. It describes a contentious confrontation between the legendary apostles Cephas/Peter and Paul. The congregation was a shining example of inter-ethnic religious fellowship, both Gentiles and Jews uniting in their devotion to Christ. They participated in common suppers, though one group restricted

---

27. Joachim Jeremias, *Jesus' Promise to the Nations*. Trans. S.H. Hooke. Studies in Biblical Theology No. 24 (London: SCM Press, 1958).

themselves to a kosher menu, while the other rejoiced in their ham sandwiches and shrimp puffs. Peter affirmed his solidarity with his newfound Gentile brethren by taking a seat at their table and, presumably, sharing their cuisine. But suddenly a contingent from James the Just, head of the Jerusalem congregation, arrived. Peter knew they were quite strict in their scruples. To avoid their censure, he quickly switched tables and menus! Noticing this, and the implied sleight to the Gentile brethren, Paul took the occasion to rebuke Peter for seeming, by his example, to disapprove the behavior of the Gentiles.

It didn't come to blows, but that wouldn't have been out of the question, as we can see in Acts chapter 21. James welcomes Paul to Jerusalem but quickly warns him he may be walking into a buzz-saw: there are thousands of Jewish Christian in the city who believe reports that Paul is teaching that continued Torah observance is no longer necessary. It is not quite clear that these reports are groundless, but when Paul appears at the Temple to publicly perform a Jewish ritual to allay the fears of these "zealots for the Torah" (21:20), the gesture backfires and those suspicious of him burst into a riot, howling for Paul's blood!

This brings us to consider another revealing aspect of the story of the Centurion's slave/son, namely that there is no suggestion that the Centurion's faith in Jesus, greater than any found among Jesus' Jewish contemporaries, is in any way incompatible with his military service. Granted, that issue is not the subject of the passage, but, then again, isn't that the point? How could it *not* be if Jesus equated discipleship with anti-militarism? If that had been part of the agenda of Jesus or of the gospel writers, shouldn't Jesus have said something like, "Well, tell you what I'll do, Captain: you quit the army and I'll heal your son. Deal?"

The same observation applies to the Acts 10–11 story of Peter and another Roman centurion, Cornelius. Peter is astonished to realize that God accepts anyone of any race, and whether or not they observe the Jewish laws. By the same implicit logic, pacifist Christians ought to be equally surprised that God poured out the Spirit even upon military officers!

Think of the story of Levi the IRS agent (Mark 2:14). Levi readily takes it for granted that his occupation is incompatible with his new faith. If pacifists were right, why don't we see Jesus and Peter expecting their centurions to quit their jobs, too?

We have already discussed, in connection with Robert Eisler, the exhortations of John the Baptist to the various groups of repentant sinners, including soldiers on the eve of war. This means that Eisler was treating the passage as a fossil of an earlier, pre-canonical portrayal of John. But now we turn to the text as part of canonical Luke: "'Soldiers also asked him, 'And we, what shall we do?' And he said to them, 'Rob no one by violence or by false accusation, and be content with your wages'" (Luke 3:14). Here was a beautiful opportunity for the Baptizer, speaking for Luke, to tell the soldiers, "Well, first, of course, you've got to throw away that sword!" But he doesn't. He only tells them not to be "bad cops." Whatever the historical John may have thought, it would seem clear that Luke did not regard military service as incompatible with righteousness. But Harnack noted a caution:

> No flight from the world is demanded, nor from one's calling. What is required is simple morality. The special mention of the soldiers is striking, however, even if we think about Jewish soldiers in the army of Herod Antipas. But Luke did not write for Jews, hence not for Jewish soldiers. This may suggest

> that he wanted to say to his gentile Christian readers that a Christian soldier demonstrates his Christian calling by not engaging in robbery and extortion. If so, this is an expression of acceptance of the military profession under this condition. One may surmise that Luke is to be understood in this way. However, it is hard to remove the objection that it is not Jesus himself who says this, but his forerunner.[28]

But to the contrary, I should say there is no substance to that objection at all. For Luke, John the Baptist is the greatest of all the prophets (Luke 7:26ff). If we can set aside Luke 3:14 because it is "merely" the teaching of John the Baptist, why not dismiss Luke 3:7–9 as well? Or the various Lukan Canticles?

The relevant question is not whether John, as depicted in Luke, is to be read as being just as authoritative as the Jesus character in Luke's script, but rather whether Luke's Baptist is, like Eisler's, a true representation of the historical John. The unnamed Baptist analog in the Slavonic Josephus is a prophet of crisis. The hour of eschatological Armageddon has come, and the Baptizer plays the role of the gold-crowned son of man in Revelation 14:14–15, summoned by a fellow angel, "Put in your sickle and reap! For the hour of reaping has come! For the harvest of the earth is fully ripe!" But John's role is quite different in Luke's gospel. As Hans Conzelmann[29] noted, for Luke, John is no longer the returned Elijah come to herald the arrival of

---

28. Adolf Harnack, *Militia Christi: The Christian Religion and the Military in the First Three Centuries*. Trans. David McInnes Gracie (Philadelphia: Fortress Press, 1981), p. 71.

29. Conzelmann, pp. 104, 114. See also Andrew J. Mattill, Jr., *Luke and the Last Things: A Perspective for the Understanding of Lukan Thought* (Dillsboro: Western Carolina Press, 1979), chapter II, "John the Baptist as a Non-Apocalyptic Preacher of Repentance," pp. 14–16.

the Christ. Luke has reconfigured the eschatological timeline: the Parousia has been delayed, probably more than once, and so Luke has deferred the expected End to some unknown future. This means Christians need no longer strive to follow a rigid and self-sacrificing interim ethic according to which one must prepare for Judgment Day and never mind everything else. The challenge for those stuck in this tired, mundane, and sinful world is to find "the relevance of an impossible ethical ideal."[30] John's exhortations to the newly baptized are promulgated as part of that agenda.[31] And thus they are the exhortations, not of John the Baptizer, but of the evangelist Luke *to his readers*. This means, of course, that they represent a bourgeois Christian ethic of the second century, and by no means an anti-militarist one.

Hans von Campenhausen[32] offers another possibility for understanding the exhortations, not as a historical report, but as aimed at the contemporary readership, though he is thinking of a different group of readers.

> [I]n the preaching of John the Baptist (Luke 3.14) . . . in so far as the soldiers were admonished to a more controlled and ordered way of life, their profession, at any rate, was not condemned, but, under certain conditions, accepted. This argument was used already in Tertullian's time by the defenders of the military service of Christians, and rightly so. The only

30. Reinhold Niebuhr, *An Interpretation of Christian Ethics* (New York: Living Age Books/Meridian Books, 1960), chapter 4, "The Relevance of an Impossible Ethical Ideal," pp. 97–126.

31. Conzelmann, p. 102.

32. Hans von Campenhausen, *Tradition and Life in the Church: Essays and Lectures in Church History*. Trans. A.V. Littledale (Philadelphia: Fortress Press, 1963), chapter 7, "Christians and the Military in the Early Church," p. 162, n. 10.

thing to notice is that the passage does not refer to Christian soldiers, and that Luke, the only one to report it, did so, probably, with a certain apologetic intention: to dissipate official misgivings about the new movement on this point.

3 Mary Had a Little Lamb
Was Jesus a Pacifist?

Apolitical Apocalypse

Some modern-era scholars have seen nothing political in Jesus as recorded in the gospels. This might be a good or a bad thing depending on how one looks at it. Rabbi Joseph Klausner,[1] generally an admirer of Jesus, regarded it as a regrettable blind spot that Jesus had nothing to say about political things, as he thus created a vacuum for the Christian Church which, having no guidance from him, defaulted into worldly politics, for instance, Caesaro-papist authoritarianism. Jesus could have prevented such abuses had he only done what Moses and Samuel and Chairman Mao did. But instead, he shrugged off any such duties: "O man, who appointed me a judge or an arbiter over you?" (Luke 12:13–14).

Liberal Protestant theologian Adolf Harnack[2] took a dif-

1. Joseph Klausner, *Jesus of Nazareth: His Life, Times, and Teaching* (New York: Macmillan, 1925).

2. Adolf Harnack, *What Is Christianity?* Trans. Thomas Bailey Saunders

ferent view of the matter. Yes, Jesus had nothing to say on governance and policy, but that is good. Had he worked out some political theory or platform, it must soon become obsolete and incompatible as times and conditions changed. So he left that task to future generations, like the king who departed for a journey, entrusting money to his servants to see what they would do with it in his absence. (Compare Matthew 25:14–30 with 1 Corinthians 3:10–15.) It might be thought that, when he began to advocate the Social Gospel of humanitarian service in the name of Jesus, Harnack forgot what he had said. But I think it was rather that he took on that responsibility that Jesus had bequeathed to future generations of disciples, and he considered the Social Gospel to be the appropriate Christian response to the conditions of his age.

Albert Schweitzer[3] saw Jesus as providing no political guidance, but for almost the opposite reason that Harnack had suggested. Jesus did not trust Christians to deal in their best Christian way with the circumstances of their future because he believed there would *be* no future. The world as we know it would soon come crashing down at the blast of the Last Trumpet and the shout of the Archangel. Politics? Why bother rear-

(New York: Harper & Row, 1957), p. 119; Harnack, "The Evangelical Social Mission in Light of the History of the Church," Chapter I., "General Attitude of the Gospel towards Social Arrangements," in Adolf Harnack and Wilhelm Herrmann, *Essays on the Social Gospel*. Trans. G.M. Craig. Crown Theological Library Vol. XVIII (London: Williams & Norgate, 1907), pp. 13–14.

3. Albert Schweitzer, *The Quest of the Historical Jesus*. Otherwise, Schweitzer shared a good bit of agreement with Harnack: he approved the general, liberal ethical stance Harnack derived from Jesus as a model for us, but he thought Harnack mistaken in ascribing it directly to Jesus. Schweitzer saw Jesus' own ethics, the "interim ethic," as more radical in both motive and application. He also agreed with Harnack that Jesus gave no thought to social reform, caring only for individual piety.

ranging the deck chairs on the *Titanic*? Any ethic must, given these constraints, be an *interim ethic*: emergency measures on the eve of the End. Extra righteousness, like turning the other cheek, or giving away your money to do the only thing left to be done with it: feeding those in imminent danger of starvation. On the one hand, you can afford to do it because there is no future to prudently provide for. On the other, you had best beef up your resume of good works because God will be checking it very soon. He's going to find out who's been naughty or nice!

Prince of Peace

So, might Jesus have been a *pacifist*, as Mennonites and Quakers think? This estimate of Jesus seems to be based upon a couple of gospel passages. The first is the famous command to turn the other cheek to get slapped after having the first one smacked (Matt. 5:39). The second is like unto it: Matthew 26:52, "All who take up the sword shall perish by the sword." Remarkably slim pickin's, no?

The first passage concerns non-retaliation in interpersonal relations. Nothing at all is said of warfare. Indeed, it appears to rule out the pacifist reading because of the specific circumstances depicted: an individual slaps you in the face. Should you return a like blow? Are we talking about a battlefield here? Did the Roman legions conquer an empire by slapping people? To count this saying as a proof text for pacifism seems ludicrous. Beyond that, it is a pretty risky inference. If I were faced with the choice of meekly yielding to some terrorist versus defending myself with counter-violence, I think the mere *possibility* that

Jesus meant to forbid self-defense would not be enough to tip the balance. I'd like better exegetical odds. How about you?

What Jesus says to Peter about the inevitable violent death of the violent man does not entirely fit the context. It is not exactly a command to renounce violence but more like a fatalistic observation like these. "The poor you have with you always" (Mark 14:7). "To him who has more, more will be given; from him who has nothing, what pittance he does have will be taken away" (Matt. 25:29; Luke 19:26). "Take no thought for the morrow; today's troubles are enough for today" (Matt. 6:34). Or think of what Jesus says about divorce: it is always a declension from God's best plan, but Jesus says not a thing about henceforth prohibiting divorce, only that even God must reckon with the stubbornness of the human heart (Mark 10:5; cf., Gen. 8:21).

I watch reruns of *The Rifleman* pretty much every day. A recurring theme is that if a man acquires a reputation as a fast gun, he will forever be plagued by challengers hoping to outdraw him, to enhance their own reputations. The only way to escape this fate is to be outgunned—killed. "Those who live by the sword will sooner or later die the same way."

It is conceivable that Jesus shared the provisional quietism of the Dead Sea Scrolls sect. They would not indulge in violence against the enemies of the Jews. "Vengeance is mine! I will repay" (Rom. 12:19). They waited with growing impatience for God to open the skies and dispatch an army of angels to deal with the pagans. But when that day arrived, the sectarians would plunge right in with sword and shield. They even had battle plans drawn up! You can read them in the *War Scroll* ("The War of the Sons of Light and the Sons of Darkness"). Is this really pacifism?

Inconvenient Genocide

Early Christians advocating pacifism had a major challenge when it came to the Old Testament tales celebrating the divinely mandated genocidal crusades against various Canaanite city-states. In order to leave nothing in doubt, the biblical authors specified that nothing and no one was to escape alive from these bloodbaths. Everything that breathed did so no longer, whether adult, child, infant, or animals! That's a strange brand of pacifism!

> Unable to find a satisfactory literal meaning for the numerous wars and acts of violence in the OT, [Origin] spiritualizes them . . . by means of allegory . . . [Accordingly,] the OT wars and battles are seen as a spiritual battle of Christ and the Christians against the evil powers and especially the demons who are the cause of sin and the things that lead to war.[4]
>
> [T]he actions of Israel of old cannot be simply emulated by Christians, and the wars of the Old Testament must be understood as having a spiritual sense if they are to be incorporated into the Christian scheme of things.[5]

This at first sounds painfully implausible, the kind of apologetics no one can offer with a straight face. But, astonishingly, in view of modern Old Testament Minimalism, there is actually something *to* it! It concerns the theologico-literary function of the pagan Canaanites. A careful reading of the books of Joshua

---

4. Robert J. Daly, Chapter 6, "Origen," in John Helgeland, Robert J. Daly, and J. Patout Burns, *Christians and the Military: The Early Experience* (Philadelphia: Fortress Press, 1985), pp. 41–42.

5. George Kalantzis, *Caesar and the Lamb: Early Christian Attitudes on War and Military Service* (Eugene: Cascade Books, 2012), p. 146.

and Judges reveals that the annihilating blitzkriegs led by Joshua, Samuel, and Saul simply cannot have happened. Not only do we lack any archaeological evidence for such destruction as these texts depict, but immediately following the completion of this wiping clean of the Canaanites, we find Joshua inventorying all the territories yet to be conquered—and it pretty much amounts to the whole seaboard (Josh. 13:1–7; Judg. 1:27–36)! That's the tip-off. That's the little red light blinking. What gives?

It may be surprising to learn (from the Old Testament itself!) that ancient Israelite religion mirrored Canaanite religion in every respect, including infant sacrifice, idol-worship, polytheism, necromancy, the profusion of local altars, you name it! There was no way of denying this. But the Israelite epic had been rewritten to pretend that Moses had already set forth the Jewish orthodoxy that had originated only recently, in the Deuteronomic Reform. But tales of the old days, the Judges, the prophets, the patriarchs, etc., were replete with unembarrassed descriptions of *Israelite* polytheism, idolatry, sacred prostitution, etc. How could *that* be if Moses had long since forbidden such nonsense? The fiction adopted by the redactors was that the Israelites already knew better but were time and again seduced into degenerate pagan ways. Oh, the prophets constantly rebuked them for it, sometimes producing short-lived repentance. The cycle played out again and again. But this is always unhistorical fiction. The stories of crushing the Canaanites were really object lessons, urging Jews no longer to tolerate the "pagan" ways, actually, of their own ancestors. This was the product of a transitional period when the religious hierarchy was trying, by carrot and stick, to propagate and enforce the new orthodoxy. It was the "Canaanite in your soul" who had to be overcome. This is exactly the guidance taken by literalistic fundamentalists, even though they do believe it all really happened.

On This Rock I Will Organize my Community

Was Jesus a community organizer? Some have thought so. John Howard Yoder, skirt-chasing Mennonite New Testament scholar,[6] floated an early version of this theory in his 1972 book *The Politics of Jesus*.[7] An Evangelical Christian, Yoder viewed Jesus in traditional theological terms plus the Anabaptist specialty of Jesus the pacifist. Yoder disliked the tendency of critics to deny certain sayings to the historical Jesus on the grounds that, as a proclaimer of the imminent Judgment Day, he could hardly have founded a church, an institution with rules of conduct and behavior such as we read in, say, the Sermon on the Mount and in Matthew chapters 18–19. Why bother, since there will soon be no ongoing world in which to govern one's mutual behavior? The problem is exactly like its Old Testament counterpart, the various Torah codes ascribed to Moses in the wilderness. They are anachronistic, predicated on Israelites already living a settled agricultural existence in Canaan. Clearly, these laws were formulated in Canaan/Israel, by Jews who lived there, to govern life and commerce there. Moses' name was borrowed to lend

6. For links to investigative news articles published in *The Elkhart Truth* about Yoder's sexual misconduct, see "John Howard Yoder's Sexual Misconduct—Part One," Peace Theology, https://peacetheology.net/john-h-yoder/john-howard-yoder%e2%80%99s-sexual-misconduct%e2%80%94part-one/.

7. John Howard Yoder, *The Politics of Jesus* (Grand Rapids: Eerdmans, 1972).

them clout. Ditto for the "church rules"[8] attributed to Jesus in the gospels.

Yoder, when not busy sexually harassing women at Goshen Biblical Seminary, came up with a way of circumventing the difficulty. He wanted *Jesus* to have said all those things, not some nameless Christian prophets or legislators. So here it is: what if Jesus viewed things as Gandhi would two thousand years later: "Be the change you want to see"? Suppose he taught a kind of "realized eschatology," creating a proto-church already in this fallen, pre-messianic age? It would be a beach head of the soon-coming kingdom of God, initiating the sort of sanctified, harmonious lifestyle that would be universal in the coming kingdom, though swimming against the current until then. You know, the cost of discipleship[9] and all that.

Yoder was not really describing what Schweitzer had called an "interim ethic," because Schweitzer figured Jesus envisioned no social dimension. Rather, repentance was a matter of "every man for himself." (Remember the deck chairs on the Titanic?) Schweitzer had factored in what Yoder didn't, namely the utter discontinuity between This Age and the Age to Come. Who needs to be warned not to lust after his neighbor's wife (Matt. 5:28) if the sons of the resurrection are like angels who neither marry nor are given in marriage (Luke 20:34–36)? Do you really need to be told not to hate or kill your neighbor (Matt. 5:21–22) when the redeemed will be one big happy family in the

8. Rudolf Bultmann, *The History of the Synoptic Tradition.* Trans. John Marsh (New York: Harper & Row, 1968), "Legal Sayings and Church Rules," pp. 130–150.

9. Dietrich Bonhoeffer, *The Cost of Discipleship.* Trans. Irmgard Booth (New York: Macmillan, 1963).

Millennium? Jewish Kabbalists[10] understood the point: the Torah could not survive into the kingdom of God without drastic transformation; otherwise, it must become a cobwebbed museum relic. Of all this Yoder seemed oblivious.

A newer version of "Jesus the community organizer" was popularized (at least within the scholarly fish tank) by Richard A. Horsley,[11] who just happened to be a community organizer himself. Coincidence? I don't have enough faith to believe that. John Dominic Crossan[12] has made this Jesus model central to his (grossly anachronistic) reconstruction of the historical Jesus and Christian origins. We find it also in Elisabeth Schüssler Fiorenza's[13] discussion of Jesus' "discipleship of equals." Though these scholars are on the opposite end of the theological spectrum from Yoder, they share his interest in vindicating various dubious gospel sayings as authentic words of Jesus. "There's something about that name!" Namely its propaganda value.

Horsley, Crossan, and the rest picture Jesus as going village

---

10. Gershom Scholem, *On the Kabbalah and Its Symbolism*. Trans. Ralph Manheim (New York: Schocken Books, 1969), chapter 2, "The Meaning of the Torah in Jewish Mysticism," pp. 32–86.

11. Richard A. Horsley, *Jesus and the Spiral of Violence: Popular Jewish Resistance in Roman Palestine* (Minneapolis: Fortress Press, 1993), chapter 8, "The Renewal of Local Community, I: Egalitarian Social Relations," pp. 209–245; chapter 9, "The Renewal of Local Community, II: Social-Economic Cooperation and Authority," pp. 246–284.

12. John Dominic Crossan, *The Historical Jesus: The Life of a Mediterranean Jewish Peasant* (San Francisco: HarperSanFrancisco, 1991), chapter 13, "Magic and Meal," pp. 303–353.

13. Elisabeth Schüssler Fiorenza, *In Memory of Her: A Feminist Theological Reconstruction of Christian Origins* (New York: Crossroad, 1984), chapter 4, "The Jesus Movement as Renewal Movement Within Judaism," section 5, "Liberation from Patriarchal Structures and the Discipleship of Equals," pp. 140–154.

to village, organizing what Latin American Liberation theologians call "base communities,"[14] something like today's "sanctuary cities," a network of effectively autonomous shadow governments in which debt amnesty would be declared, patriarchal families and hierarchical authority would be dissolved, and Roman courts would be boycotted. One thinks inevitably of the People's Front of Judea in *Monty Python's The Life of Brian*.[15] It is all a lattice of transparently spurious Jesus quotes that Bultmann wouldn't have touched with a ten-foot pole, which are then reinterpreted according to a modern Leftist agenda. Somebody apparently never read Henry J. Cadbury's classic book *The Peril of Modernizing Jesus*.[16]

Crossan envisions Jesus getting his sympathizers to give their money to a common fund, as in the early chapters of the Book of Acts, and imperiously declaring the Levitical laws segregating lepers null and void, inviting them, stinking mummy bandages and all, to share the supposedly joyous table fellowship of "commensality." He and Horsley sound like they are describing the behaviors of a Melanesian Cargo Cult,[17] except that those modern apocalyptic social movements did all these things

14. Ernesto Cardinal, *The Gospel in Solentename* (Maryknoll: Orbis Books, 1978). Such a radical, autonomous community is well portrayed in the unintentionally hilarious 1969 Elvis movie *Change of Habit* in which a radicalized nun, with no authorization, declares a debt amnesty for everybody in the ghetto in which she serves.

15. Graham Chapman, John Cleese, Terry Gilliam, Eric Idle, Terry Jones, Michael Palin, *Monty Python's The Life of Brian (of Nazareth)* (New York: Ace Books, 1979).

16. Henry J. Cadbury, *The Peril of Modernizing Jesus* (New York: Macmillan, 1937).

17. Peter Worsley, *The Trumpet Shall Sound: A Study of "Cargo" Cults in Melanesia* (New York: Schocken Books, 1968).

in order to trash the mores of this age, which is passing away (1 Cor. 7:29–31), and to exhaust their worldly resources, burning all bridges to the passing order. Those without the faith to do this must be shut out of salvation. In other words, they were by no means trying to set the ground rules for a new ongoing society to replace the old one. It was, again, an *interim* ethic.

But Albert Schweitzer was right on something else, too. In *The Quest of the Historical Jesus*, Schweitzer exposed the many previous historical Jesus reconstructions as mirror images of their authors' theological and social views. Jesus as a ventriloquist dummy. And Jesus the community organizer is the new Charlie McCarthy.

Persecution and Pacifism

The question of Christian martyrdom is closely connected with our central theme of Christians in the Roman army. This is because opponents of Christian soldiering, e.g., Tertullian, loved to hold up such martyrs as proof that Christians should stay away from the barracks, lest they be forced to compromise the Christian ethic with Roman orders to kill. When push comes to shove, why not stay safely on the sidelines, piously praying?

Candida Moss[18] defines persecution and martyrdom as the respective infliction and suffering of violence upon members of a religious group because of the victims' religious identity. And though the same Greek word (*dioko*) lies behind both our words

---

18. Candida Moss, *The Myth of Persecution How Early Christians Invented a Story of Martyrdom* (New York: Harper One, 2013).

"persecution" and "prosecution," Moss argues that it is vital that we distinguish between the two. Sometimes, as she shows, the ancient Romans merely (at least from their own point of view) prosecuted Christians because Christians stubbornly refused to obey Roman laws (e.g., mandating the offering of incense to the divine spirit of Caesar) because of certain unintended consequences. Sacrificing to Caesar seemed no more to Rome than the Pledge of Allegiance does to traditionalist Americans today, who take offense at those who refuse to salute the flag. Roman officials could not be expected to anticipate the offense. It was offense taken (by Christians) more than offense given (by Romans). And, though Moss does not otherwise trust the accuracy of the ostensible reporting in ancient accounts of the martyrs' courtroom dramas, she seems to take literally the bratty defiance of Christians who sometimes even refused to state their names for the record. They thought they were shouldering the cross of Jesus when they were actually just carrying a cross-sized chip on the shoulder. They would have seemed like today's Code Pink activists or Wall Street Occupiers: self-righteous nuisances and hooligans. In short, they appear to have been asking for it. And some literally did ask for it, volunteering for execution so as to win the best seats in heaven. Here one thinks of the Al-Qaida slogan, "You love life; we love death."

Moss does not deny that ancient Romans did execute some Christians because they *were* Christians, but not *merely* because of it. Rather, as Christians, disdaining any authority but that of a rival king, Jesus (Acts 17:7), they were refusing to abide by the prevalent social contract whereby the survival of the empire depended upon religio-civic piety whose figurehead was the emperor. As Moss describes it, it sounds as if the pagan Romans had their own version of the Deuteronomic theology: apostasy among the chosen people will cause them to forfeit divine protection. One may wonder if they would have freaked out at the disloyalty of a tiny sect of crackpots, but apparently, they did.

But how much and how often were Christians either persecuted or prosecuted? Moss arrives at a rather modest estimate of a measly dozen years, during the reign of Diocletian, and even then there was a lot less to it than we have been led (mainly by the institutional propagandist Eusebius) to believe. It is no news among scholars that the vast ocean of martyrdom stories dating from the fourth century (their heyday) are grossly fictive. But Moss carefully examines even the handful of second-century accounts, beginning with *The Martyrdom of Polycarp* and has no trouble demonstrating that these, too, are either obviously bogus or at least have been so redacted and idealized from a later standpoint that whatever core of truth they may contain is not retrievable and may not exist at all. It's not exactly failing to see the forest for the trees. It's more like finding there *is* no longer any forest because all the trees have been cut down.

Martyr accounts started to flourish once the Diocletian trouble was past, and for reasons of ecclesiastical power politics. Eusebius, a great cataloguer of martyr-fictions, tended to meld the (real and imagined) pagan persecutors of the past with their supposed successors in his own day, the so-called heretics, both of them Satan's agents to subvert and to destroy the One True Church. This equation allowed him to invoke the martyrs as endorsing the theological opinions of Eusebius' own party. For instance, Eusebius tells his readers that the blessed martyrs of Lyons, just before they were killed, petitioned the bishop of Rome to name Irenaeus to succeed the bishop about to bite the dust. Moss early on mentions the stale argument of Christian apologists that Jesus must really have risen from the dead because the apostles would scarcely have yielded up their lives for a falsehood (though we have no evidence at all as to how they may have died, whether by boiling in oil, by skiing accidents, or via auto-erotic asphyxiation). She warns us that this bad argument will be found writ large over the history of martyrdom, and this is what she means: Eusebius and the other spin-doctors invoked the testimony of martyrs and confessors[19] to establish orthodoxy. If these saintly folks attested to the truth of our faith (and *not yours!*), this must mean they (i.e., *we*) were right!

It is a bit surprising that Moss does not make more of Ignatius of Antioch in this regard than she does. In a couple of footnotes, she does mention the Ignatian Epistles as examples of a martyr's clout being used to reinforce the authority of the bishops. And, as such, Ignatius is an even better example of what she is talking about than is Eusebius. But, more than this, since the Ignatian corpus is almost certainly a set of bogus pseudepigrapha, it serves as a prime example of the sort of pious fabrication that forms the martyrdom tradition. Especially given that the Antiochene martyr is portrayed in these writings as a suicidal fanatic who just cannot wait to have the shreds of his flesh picked from the teeth of the lions who will munch on him in the Coliseum.

And, speaking of forged letters, Moss is altogether too forgiving of implausibility when she takes as authentic the famous 117th letter of Pliny the Younger to his boss Trajan. This

19. Confessors were those who boldly witnessed to their faith even under the threat of death, though, one way or another, they escaped execution. Needless to say, they had earned considerable clout among the brethren!

is a transparent bit of apologetic, wherein an outsider, even a persecutor, is made to praise the very objects of his wrath as not deserving it, as well as attesting to their fantastic success: so many have deserted paganism that the meat markets are stuck with the steaks that used to keep the sacrificial altars running with blood. No record of Roman policy toward Christians, this letter merely uses literary ventriloquism for Christian self-praise.

Similarly, I suspect Moss is being too easy on Tacitus' account of Nero's persecution of Christians in the first century. She winds up minimizing the importance of it anyway, but is it not worth mentioning that some view the relevant passage as a later interpolation since no Christian till Eusebius mentions this alleged persecution, even though it would have come in quite handy?

Moss shows how ostensible trial records in martyr accounts do not really conform to the legal patterns on record in actual trial transcripts from the ancient world, and that the martyrs are often depicted as standing up for much later theological beliefs than prevailed in the era in which the scenes are set. It has long been evident to biblical critics that the same applies in spades to the gospel trial narratives. What? The Sanhedrin trying Jesus on Passover Eve? Not a chance. And finding him guilty of blasphemy for his messianic claims? There was nothing blasphemous about Jesus, Bar Kochba, or anybody else claiming to be the Messiah (though of course they might be mistaken). No, the "son of God" business surely reflects the later Christian Christology, not of a Jewish king, but of a divine being. The gospel trial scenes are no more historical than the fanciful martyrologies.

We must, however, wonder if the gospels do not give us more evidence of early persecution than Moss allows for. Do not the texts contain plenty of warnings that Christians must be prepared to be dragged before hostile magistrates, to be willing to carry their crosses as Jesus did, etc.? Moss mentions these texts, but her reading is that these ancient Christians were mistaken in their expectations. But that seems to me too facile. Granted, Jesus issued no such warnings; they are anachronistic for his day, since they assume that Christians are already a distinct, outlaw sect. But isn't the rule that all such "predictions" are made after the fact, to create the impression that events in the writer's own day were already foreseen? We wouldn't be reading them at all unless somebody were saying, albeit fictively, "I told you so." So the axiom of historical interconnection bids us determine when such persecutions reared their ugly heads and then to date the relevant texts there (the *Sitz-im-Leben*). Maybe the gospels are even later than some of us had thought.

One radical hunch begets another: is it possible that the reports about the third-century persecutors demanding that Christians hand over their sacred books should be understood along the same lines that Old Testament Minimalists understand 4 Ezra 14, where the seer reminds God how, apparently during the Babylonian capture of Jerusalem in 567 BCE, "thy Law has been burned, and so no one knows the things that have been done or will be done by thee" (v. 21) and asks that he may be supernaturally inspired to replace the lost 24 books of the canon (vv. 22–45)? Is not this passage an attempt to create a false ancient pedigree for books written, *de novo*, in one's own day? And dare we consider whether various New Testament writings were likewise composed as ostensible "replacements" for hypothetical apostolic scriptures that actually had no previous existence? That would sure explain all those apparently anachronistic references to persecution.

Finally, if Eusebius trumped up the myth of a long age of Christian martyrdom in order to advance the interests of his preferred brand of Christianity, it seems equally likely that Candida Moss's demolition effort has political motivations of its own. She warns that the long-cherished paranoia of Christians who imagine themselves the constant targets of Satan and his agents contributes to a political climate in which modern Christians refuse to take seriously the reasoned opinions of ideological opponents. She bemoans the shrill protests of Catholics Rick Santorum and Newt Gingrich and Presbyterian Ann Coulter who compare opposition by liberal politicians and media to Roman persecution of their ancient co-religionists. But one may wonder if Moss's use of the persecution trope as a weapon of accusation against these conservatives is not itself a mirror-image version of the tactic she decries.

Let's Be (Jacob) Frank: Realized Eschatology

Martyr pacifism was an attempt to live in the present as if it were the future millennium, which it supposedly *was*, albeit in "mustard seed" form. Perhaps in some way the clearest explanation of this metaphor might be the sect of Jacob Frank[20] in eighteenth-century Eastern Europe. A follower of the failed seventeenth-century Messiah Sabbatai Sevi, Frank came to believe that he was Sabbatai's successor, a second Messiah and, like

---

20. Pawel Maciejko, *The Mixed Multitude: Jacob Frank and the Frankist Movement 1755–1816* (Philadelphia: University of Pennsylvania Press, 2011).

his predecessor, a divine Incarnation. Sabbatai had proclaimed the imminent dawning of the Messianic Age and boasted that he would confront the Turkish sultan and get him to convert to Judaism. Instead, when threatened with execution, Sabbatai renounced Judaism and converted to Islam![21] Most of his adherents dispersed, disillusioned. Nobody, it seems, accosted them on the road back to Emmaus. But others continued the movement, adjusting their expectations to the harsh new realities. Jacob Frank inherited this remarkable faith, reasoning that the Messianic Age had indeed arrived on schedule, albeit in an outwardly invisible form. It would take a good dose of faith to see it.[22]

This meant that believers were free to celebrate (orgiastically!)[23] the New Age, but from concealment, behind closed doors in the dark of night. You see, their eschatological doctrine included the belief of many Jewish mystics that, in the Messianic Age, the text of the Torah would be changed by the sudden appearance of a hitherto-hidden letter in this and that word.[24] What kind of changes? Of the 613 scriptural commandments, by far most were negative, prohibitions, "thou shalt nots." But all sin would be eradicated in the Messianic Age, so there could be

21. Gershom G. Scholem, *Sabbatai Sevi the Mystical Messiah.* Trans. R.J. Zvi Werblowsky. Bollingen Series XCIII (Princeton: Princeton University Press, 1973.

22. What a striking example of Berger and Luckman's "finite provinces of meaning"! Peter L. Berger and Thomas Luckmann, *The Social Construction of Reality: A Treatise in the Sociology of Knowledge* (Garden City: Doubleday Anchor Books, 1967), pp. 25–26.

23. Gershom G. Scholem, "Redemption through Sin." Trans. Hillel Halkin. In Scholem, *The Messianic Idea in Judaism and Other Essays on Jewish Spirituality* (New York: Schocken Books, 1971), pp. 78–141.

24. Gershom Scholem, "The Meaning of the Torah in Jewish Mysticism," In Scholem, *Messianic Idea in Judaism* pp. 80–82.

no sins to prohibit. In fact, whatever had previously been forbidden would now be commanded! Yikes! This, you didn't do in public! The seed was germinating unseen to the eye for the present, but one day it would blossom forth for all to see, and earth would become a new and universal Eden. Any outsider would say this was just a fancy way of saying you were pretending the Kingdom had come, even though most of the hours of the day you couldn't afford to play. At any rate, it is becoming clear how "hiding" your faith was closely connected to the delay of eschatological hope. One day (soon?) "there will be no more night" (Rev. 21:25) and, equally, no need to hide your light under a bushel (Matt. 5:15).

Constantinianism was, finally, the real-world blossoming of the eschatological hopes. But even though the Kingdom of God had dawned with Constantine and Theodosius, it could not entirely slough off the ambiguities of this-worldly existence and thus was stuck with compromise. And that meant, for many, that eventually you got tired of the game and faced your mundane responsibilities, putting away childish things. "The opinions of the Christians of the first three centuries . . . were usually formed without regard to the necessities of civil or political life; but when the Church obtained ascendancy, it was found necessary speedily to modify them."[25]

Mere Formality

Elaine Pagels draws a connection between early Christian mar-

25. W.E.H. Lecky, *History of European Morals*, in Cadoux, p. 66.

tyrdom and belief in Christ's real, fleshly incarnation.[26] Some who favored Docetism (from *dokeo*, "to seem"), the doctrine that Jesus was pure spirit, like a hologram, rejected martyrdom as futile grandstanding. Since Jesus had not actually suffered and died, why should Christians? By contrast, it is no accident that Bishop Ignatius (possibly pseudepigraphic) author of the Ignatian Epistles, both relished the prospect of his own impending martyrdom in the arena *and* insistently defended the doctrine of Jesus' gory suffering and death. One thinks of Peregrinus the Cynic philosopher and sometime Christian apostle, who arranged for a great bonfire to be lit and announced he would walk right into it. He did, and, as a joke, the satirist Lucian started swearing he had observed an eagle (the new host of Peregrinus' spirit) rising from the inferno into the heavens![27]

I should think this widespread attitude qualifies as a robust alternative position on martyrdom, something often occasioned by Christian soldiers' conscientious objections. Yet conventional discussions of early Christian pacifism never mention it. Why? Simply because even modern-era theological historians cannot bring themselves to see beyond the Eusebian paradigm. It simply does not occur to them that Gnostic and Docetic "heretics" were Christians, too! We see the same obliviousness when apologists affirm, as against form criticism, that there is no evidence that "the early Christians" fabricated sayings and attributed them to Jesus to increase their authority. Obviously, they just aren't thinking of Gnostic texts that are filled to the brim with

---

26. Elaine Pagels, *The Gnostic Gospels* (New York: Random House, 1979), chapter IV, "The Passion and the Persecution of Christians," pp. 70–101.

27. Here, who will not be moved to think of Daffy Duck's historic performance as "the Great Explodo," a stunt he warned he could perform but once?

spurious "Jesus" material, e.g., *Pistis Sophia*, *The Dialogue of the Savior*, the *Books of Jeu*, etc. It's like fundamentalist Protestants who don't count Roman Catholics as "Christians."

But this is not the only reason Gnostics avoided trouble by denying their Christian identity. Saying 13 of the Gospel of Thomas tells us a revealing story.

> Jesus said to his disciples: "Make a comparison to me and tell me who I am like." Simon Peter said to him: "You are like a righteous angel." Matthew said to him: "You are like a wise man of understanding." Thomas said to him: "Master, my mouth will in no way permit me to say who you are like." Jesus said: "I am not your master, because you have drunk, you have become drunk, from the bubbling spring which I have measured out." And he took him, went aside, and told him three things. Now when Thomas returned to his companions, they asked him: "What did Jesus say to you?" Thomas said to them: "If I told you even one of the things he said to me, you would pick up stones and throw them at me; and a fire would erupt from the stones and consume you!"

I dare say this means one thing: those possessing the esoteric knowledge (*gnosis*) of the Gnostic illuminati must keep it to themselves unless asked by earnest inquirers (like the Rich Young Ruler of Matthew 19:20: "What do I still lack?"). Otherwise, it's none of the outsiders' damn business! Why? "Do not feed consecrated food to dogs, nor throw your pearls before swine, lest they trample them underfoot, then turn and attack you" (Matt. 7:6). That is, you must know what will happen if you tell common Christian believers what you really think. You already know how they must react. Your precious truth must burn like blasphemy in *their* ears, and *you* will wind up burning at the stake! Great! They will have murdered the innocent, and you will be the one who goaded them into it! So keep your mouth shut! The Sufi mystic al-Hallaj (858–922) found this out the hard way when he went about the city, half-dazed with religious ecstasy, telling one and all, "I am the Truth!" People, orthodox Sunni Muslims, naturally thought he was presumptuously announcing himself as Allah incarnate. The reviews were not good. Let us not spare ourselves the grisly details. Here is Robert Payne's colorful description.[28]

> First, his skull was smashed; then he was scourged; then his hands and feet were cut off; then the body was roped to the gibbet and tar was applied to the bleeding stumps to prevent him from bleeding to death. . . . Then the sword descended, and his head was struck off. [. . .] Some of his followers believe, as Muhammadans believe of Jesus, that he was not crucified, but a semblance or image of him was crucified instead.

Though revered as a holy martyr, many said it was his own fault for profaning the truth by speaking it to those incapable of grasping it.

Doubtless many soldiers, secretly Christians, pursued the same strategy among their Zeus- and Mithras-worshipping comrades-in-arms. Why make unnecessary trouble by blabbing your faith? Tertullian[29] relates the voluntary "outing" of a Christian soldier who just could not keep his secret faith to himself

---

28. Robert Payne, *The Holy Sword: The Story of Islam from Muhammad to the Present* (New York: Collier Books, 1962), p. 220.

29. Tertullian, "On the Crown/Chaplet," chapter 1 http://www.earlychristianwritings.com/text/tertullian04.html.

any longer.

> Very lately it happened thus: while the bounty of our most excellent emperors was dispensed in the camp, the soldiers, laurel-crowned, were approaching. One of them, more a soldier of God, more steadfast than the rest of his brethren, who had imagined that they could serve two masters, his head alone uncovered, the useless crown in his hand—already even by that peculiarity known to every one as a Christian—was nobly conspicuous.
>
> Accordingly, all began to mark him out, jeering him at a distance, gnashing on him near at hand. The murmur is wafted to the tribune when the person had just left the ranks. The tribune at once puts the question to him, Why are you so different in your attire? He declared that he had no liberty to wear the crown with the rest. Being urgently asked for his reasons, he answered, I am a Christian. O soldier! boasting thyself in God. Then the case was considered and voted on; the matter was remitted to a higher tribunal; the offender was conducted to the prefects. At once he put away the heavy cloak, his disburdening commenced; he loosed from his foot the military shoe, beginning to stand upon holy ground; and he gave up the sword, which was not necessary either for the protection of our Lord; from his hand likewise dropped the laurel crown; and now, purple-clad with the hope of his own blood, shod with the preparation of the gospel, girt with the sharper word of God, completely equipped in the apostles' armour, and crowned more worthily with the white crown of martyrdom, he awaits in prison the largess of Christ. *Thereafter adverse judgments began to be passed upon his conduct—whether on the part of Christians I do not know, for those of the heathen are not different—as if he were headstrong and rash, and too eager to die, because, in being taken to task about a mere matter of dress, he brought trouble on the bearers of the* Name,—he, for-

> sooth, alone brave among so many soldier-brethren, he alone a Christian. It is plain that as they have rejected the prophecies of the Holy Spirit, they are also purposing the refusal of martyrdom. So they murmur that a peace so good and long is endangered for them.

If we may trust Tertullian's account, it becomes plain that there were many Christian troops who found it the best path to cherish their faith in secret, letting their good deeds serve as their witness, and they were indignant that this apparent glory-hound was suddenly going to ruin things for all of them by making a spectacle of himself and forcing a hitherto-dormant issue. Thus, when Tertullian describes "the" Christian stance of pacifistic non-cooperation, he nonetheless reveals that plenty of Christians in fact believed otherwise. He "wins" his argument simply by disqualifying them as false Christians whose views therefore do not count.

But what *were* their views, or, if you like, their rationalizations for silently serving in an army whose every uniform detailing and group ritual was permeated with mythological polytheism and Caesar-worship? "And in a very clear way, [Tertullian] even shows us the scriptural proofs which are used by the representatives of the opposite viewpoint."[30] To wit: "And yet Moses carried a rod, and Aaron wore a buckle, and John [the Baptist] is girt with leather, and Joshua the son of Nun leads a line of march; and the people warred."[31]

We have already noted that Christian soldiers liked to appeal to the centurion whose faith Jesus praised as greater than

---

30. Harnack, *Militia Christi*, p. 77.
31. Tertullian, *On Idolatry*, chapter 19.

that of any Jew, as well as Cornelius in Acts 10–11. The narratives give not the slightest hint that their career occupations were incompatible with their Christian stance. But surely they must have taken their greatest comfort from the story of Naaman, the Syrian general who was grateful to Elisha for curing his leprosy (2 Kings chapter 5). Naaman, now switching allegiance to the Israelite deity Yahweh, asks the prophet for special permission to accompany his feeble monarch into the temple of the Syrian god Rimmon. Though he would, to all outward appearances, seem to be a Rimmon worshipper himself, he would continue to do his duty to his king. Elisha readily agrees. Was not this precisely the dilemma which Christians in the Roman army faced? And would not the same casuistry apply?

Or, to jump over again to the New Testament, might we not understand these Christian legionaries as being like the "stronger brethren" in Corinth? Remember, most of the difficulty Christians faced, a dilemma Tertullian harped on, stemmed from the "idolatrous" character of certain accoutrement of the Roman army uniform, including decorations. Oaths to serve the emperor, pledging absolute loyalty and obedience, seemed to constitute a distinct religion, and of course, a pagan one at that. How could sincere Christians possibly divide their loyalties? How could they serve two masters? I believe the situation they faced was precisely analogous to that discussed in 1 Corinthians chapters 8 and 10.

Corinthian Christians were divided over whether one might accept dinner invitations from pagan friends, relatives, or business colleagues if the venue was a local fellowship hall attached to a pagan temple, or in the non-Christian's home if the meat had been offered in pagan sacrifice. That is, if there was so much leftover meat after the priests received their share of the sacrifice, they would sell the remainder in the public marketplace. Your host might have purchased the steaks there. Just as Diaspora Jews would tithe what they bought at the butcher shop just in case the kosher butcher had neglected to do so, what was the Christian dinner guest to do if the steak had previously been consecrated to Apollo? On the off chance that this had happened, the "weaker" brother or sister would tell the host, "Uh . . . just salad for me tonight, thank you."

But the "stronger" Christians simply would not care. They were gustatorial "Gnostics" who rejoiced in the knowledge that Apollo and the whole gang didn't exist—"not nobody, not no how!" So *what* if some Greek-speaking witch doctor had waved the steak around in the air, chanting some holy gibberish.[32] We know they thought this, because Origin explicitly condemns their opinion. He "castigates those Christians who would propose that participating in pagan worship is not morally reprehensible since the Christian knows that these gods do not exist, and therefore one is free of the moral consequence."[33]

You see, the weaker brother was *weak in faith*. He was giving too much credit to the false gods he professed, as a Christian, to believe were not real after all. But if you fear them, doesn't that mean you, on some level, *do* believe in them? Being a weaker brother was hyper-scrupulosity. 1 Corinthians chapters 8 and 10 stand side by side as the two opposing sides in a debate. Chapter

32. It's just like the *Sopranos* episode where Tony, grateful for a favor done him by his next-door neighbor, gives him a box of fine Cuban cigars. His friend is delighted but hesitant, saying, "But these are illegal!" Tony shrugs it off and says, "They're cigars." End of story, because that's finally what it comes down to.

33. Kalantzis, p. 145.

8 is the "stronger brother" view, while chapter 10 represents that of the weaker brother. Chapter 9 has been inserted as a buffer so the reader will be less likely to notice the flat contradiction. (This is but one of many signs that 1 Corinthians is a composite document containing various "Pauline" viewpoints.)

The Christian soldiers against whom Tertullian polemicizes were the stronger brothers. To them, a piece of headgear was just an ornament. Make it any way you want! Put a likeness of the emperor's behind on it if you want! I have to offer a pinch of incense to Caesar's spirit? Fine. You got Sandalwood? Swearing oaths to the emperor was like the everyday practice of signing a contract that called on pagan deities to witness it: nothing serious. A pure formality. Diaspora Jews did it all the time, as many ancient papyri attest. Besides, 1 Timothy 2:2 urges Christians to pray for the emperor, and this is repeated by Origen, etc., but Revelation 5:8 says the offering of incense to God is prayer. It would have been a very thin line in the minds of Christian soldiers: they might have been happy enough to offer incense to Caesar, considering it a prayer to their own God for Caesar's welfare.

A striking sequence of dialogue preserved in another martyr account suggests that many Roman officers did not relish the duty of executing Christian soldiers just because of their religious convictions. If any Christians decided not to make an issue of their faith, instead merely going through the empty motions, many of their pagan superiors were happy enough to play the same game of pretend.

> "Julius," said Maximus the prefect, "I see that you are a wise and serious person. You will receive a generous bonus if you

> will take my advice and sacrifice to the gods."
>
> "I will not do what you wish," answered Julius, "lest I incur an eternal penalty."
>
> "If you think it a sin," answered the prefect Maximus, "let me take the blame. I am the one who is forcing you, so that you may not give impression of having consenting voluntarily. Afterwards you can go home in peace, you will pick up your ten-year bonus, and no one will ever trouble you again. [. . .] I counsel you out of pity," said Maximus, "that you sacrifice and continue to live with us." (*The Martyrdom of Julian the Veteran*)

There is something a bit disturbing about the zeal of martyrs who provoked their own persecution. No reader of the Ignatian epistles can fail to cringe at the author's eagerness to be torn limb from limb by hungry lions in the Roman arena. Was the aspiring martyr just looking for a way out of this cold, cruel world? It appears so. Martyrdom was the express elevator to heaven: "Let me be eaten by the wild beasts, through whom I can reach the presence of God" (Ignatius to the Romans 4:1)[34] But then again, it goes a bit deeper than that. I think of Denis de Rougemont's fascinating book *Love in the Western World*.[35] In it he explains the origin of our Western mystique of romantic love as an attempt to escape the routine character of committed monogamy with all its mundane responsibilities. Having a secret affair creates what Berger and Luckmann call a "finite province

---

34. Edgar J. Goodspeed, trans., *The Apostolic Fathers: An American Translation* (New York: Harper and Brothers, 1950), p. 222.

35. Denis de Rougement, *Love in the Western World*. Trans. Montgomery Belgion (Garden City: Doubleday Anchor Books, 1957).

of meaning,"[36] a "little zone"[37] of transcendence, an island of freedom, albeit one that requires cheating and transgression. Even though the illicit lovers know their affair cannot end well and, at least in literature, may even finish in death, it is a "great escape" into a real world of lived fantasy. Why do couples like Antony and Cleopatra, Tristan and Isolde, Romeo and Juliet, tend toward death? Not just because theirs are cautionary tales, but because death is like the hoped-for heaven of the martyrs. The only alternative "world" of total (because negative) freedom, of course, is *death*.

Jihadi suicide bombers are paying for the necessary ticket to the imaginary heaven with plenty of *houris* and white grapes for the righteous. They say to us, "You love life; we love death," but that's not really what they're thinking. What they prefer to this dreary, mundane existence is the cosmic bunny club they expect to find on the other side of the Gates of Death. What a pity if there turns out to be no theme park on the other side because there *is* no other side. And then the question presents itself: what if this world looks so shabby and crummy because we insist on comparing it with an invisible world of perfect stimulation and satisfaction that exists only to make us disappointed with this world, the only one we've got. Maybe Nagarjuna was right: so what if the soap bubble must shortly pop? Enjoy its rainbow colors while they last. Such enjoyments are the most precious precisely because they are so finite and fleeting.

While many early Christians were quite happy to do their hitch in the Roman legions (a volunteer army), others were busy

---

36. *Berger and Luckmann, Social Construction of Reality*, pp. 25–26.

37. Thomas Ligotti, "Dream of a Mannikin," in Ligotti, *Songs of a Dead Dreamer* (Albuquerque: Silver Scarab Press, 1985), p. 77.

coming up with theological reasons for staying safely at home.

> Celsus complains that the Christians were shirking their civic duties by refusing to take part in public or military life.... Like Tertullian, he argues that Christians by their prayers and good lives combat the devils and evil spirits which cause dissension and war, and that they thus fulfil their obligations to the empire.[38]

We can pretty well guess what Romans thought when they heard this! "So you folks are fighting Rome's enemies with the weapon of good vibes! Well, I guess that means we don't have to worry about those hirsute barbarians eating away at the borders!" Really, what is the difference between the efforts of these "prayer warriors" and those of the John Prum Cargo Cult in New Guinea, whose members sought to turn the tables on Western Imperialists by emulating them and copying their technology. The trouble was, they naturally had no idea how modern weaponry worked! They drilled, marching with broomstick rifles on their shoulders and pretended to communicate with radios made of orange crates with buttons attached to the front for dials. In both cases, we see what anthropologists call "imitative magic."

38. Daly, "Origen," p. 40.

4 Sacred King of Kings

The Christology of the New Testament seems to match closely the ancient Sacred King mythology that undergirded Middle Eastern monarchies. This implies Christians first deemed Jesus an actual (would-be) king.

Ancient Israelite religion was polytheistic.[1] As we read in Deuteronomy 32:7–9, some time in the misty past, El Elyon (= God Most High), the chief deity had a total of seventy sons, godlings. He decided to create the human race and made sure there were enough nations in it that each of the Sons of God would have his own fiefdom, his own people to worship and serve him, while each deity would protect his people, render justice, supply prosperity and answer their prayers. One of these gods claimed the Hebrews. His name was Yahweh (or Jehovah).

Remember the days of old,

1. Margaret Barker, *The Great Angel: A Study of Israel's Second God* (Louisville: Westminster/John Knox Press, 1992), chapter 1, "The Son of God," pp. 4–11.

> consider the years of many generations;
> ask your father, and he will show you;
> your elders, and they will tell you.
> When Elyon gave to the nations their inheritance,
> when he separated the sons of men,
> he fixed the bounds of the peoples
> according to the number of the sons of God.
> For Yahweh's portion is his people,
> Jacob his allotted heritage.

The day came when a threat arose against the gods. The primordial Chaos Dragons Leviathan, Nehushtan, Rahab, Behemoth, etc. rose to threaten the gods. By analogy with the cognate mythologies of neighboring countries, these Dragons may be understood as the parents or creators of the gods, making the myth one of generational conflict. We see the same dynamic, e.g., in Greek myth, where Zeus overthrows the Titans, including his father Kronos.

The gods shiver with fear until Yahweh, the young and virile god of thunder and of war, steps forward (as does his Babylonian counterpart Marduk, AKA Bel) and offers a deal: he will make short work of the Chaos Dragon—*if* the gods will agree to make him their new king. He can do what the elderly potentate Elyon, the white-bearded Ancient of Days, cannot. Perhaps once he would have been up to the task, but no more. So they agree. The Bible contains poetic fragments about the cosmic battle and the victory of Yahweh, who crushed the seven Hydra-heads of Leviathan/Rahab.

> God my King is from of old,
> working salvation in the midst of the earth.
> Thou didst divide the sea by thy might;

thou didst break the heads of the dragons on the waters.
Thou didst crush the heads of Leviathan,
thou didst give him as food for the creatures of the wilderness.

Thou didst cleave open springs and brooks;
thou didst dry up ever-flowing streams.
Thine is the day, thine also the night;
thou hast established the luminaries and the sun.
Thou hast fixed all the bounds of the earth;
thou hast made summer and winter.

(Psalm 74:12–17)

Let the heavens praise thy wonders, O Yahweh,
thy faithfulness in the assembly of the holy ones!
For who in the skies can be compared to Yahweh?
Who among the sons of God is like Yahweh,
a god feared in the council of the holy ones,
great and terrible above all that are round about him?
O Yahweh Sabaoth,
who is mighty as thou art, O Yahweh,
with thy faithfulness round about thee?
Thou dost rule the raging of the sea;
when its waves rise, thou stillest them.
Thou didst crush Rahab like a carcass,
thou didst scatter thy enemies with thy mighty arm.
The heavens are thine, the earth also is thine;
the world and all that is in it, thou hast founded them.
The north and the south, thou hast created them;
Tabor and Hermon joyously praise thy name.
Thou hast a mighty arm;
strong is thy hand, high thy right hand.

(Psalm 89:5–13)

Note the pattern in these two psalms. Three elements appear in each, and not randomly, though it may appear that way before you know about the myth presupposed there. First, there is Yahweh's kingship. Second is the way he attained it: by destroying the Chaos monsters. And third, his ownership (creation) of all of nature.

> Can you draw out Leviathan with a fishhook,
> or press down his tongue with a cord?
> Can you put a rope in his nose,
> or pierce his jaw with a hook?
> Will he make many supplications to you?
> Will he speak to you soft words?
> Will he make a covenant with you
> to take him for your servant for ever?
> Will you play with him as with a bird,
> or will you put him on a leash for your maidens?
> Will traders bargain over him?
> Will they divide him up among the merchants?
> Can you fill his skin with harpoons,
> or his head with fishing spears?
> Lay hands on him;
> think of the battle; you will not do it again!
>
> Behold, the hope of a man is disappointed;
> he is laid low even at the sight of him.
> No one is so fierce that he dares to stir him up.
> Who then is he that can stand before me?
> Who has given to me, that I should repay him?
> Whatever is under the whole heaven is mine.
>
> I will not keep silence concerning his limbs,
> or his mighty strength, or his goodly frame.

Who can strip off his outer garment?
  Who can penetrate his double coat of mail?
Who can open the doors of his face?
  Round about his teeth is terror.
His back is made of rows of shields,
  shut up closely as with a seal.
One is so near to another
  that no air can come between them.
They are joined one to another;
  they clasp each other and cannot be separated.
His sneezings flash forth light,
  and his eyes are like the eyelids of the dawn.
Out of his mouth go flaming torches;
  sparks of fire leap forth.
Out of his nostrils comes forth smoke,
  as from a boiling pot and burning rushes.
His breath kindles coals,
  and a flame comes forth from his mouth.
In his neck abides strength,
  and terror dances before him.
The folds of his flesh cleave together,
  firmly cast upon him and immovable.
His heart is hard as a stone,
  hard as the nether millstone.
When he raises himself up the mighty are afraid;
  at the crashing they are beside themselves.
Though the sword reaches him, it does not avail;
  nor the spear, the dart, or the javelin.
He counts iron as straw,
  and bronze as rotten wood.
The arrow cannot make him flee;
  for him slingstones are turned to stubble.
Clubs are counted as stubble;
  he laughs at the rattle of javelins.

His underparts are like sharp potsherds;
he spreads himself like a threshing sledge on the mire.
He makes the deep boil like a pot;
he makes the sea like a pot of ointment.
Behind him he leaves a shining wake;
one would think the deep to be hoary.
Upon earth there is not his like,
a creature without fear.
He beholds everything that is high;
he is king over all the sons of pride.

(Job chapter 41)

In that day Yahweh with his hard and great and strong sword will punish Leviathan the fleeing serpent, Leviathan the twisting serpent, and he will slay the dragon that is in the sea.

(Isaiah 27:1)

The pillars of heaven tremble,
and are astounded at his rebuke.
By his power he stilled the sea;
by his understanding he smote Rahab.
By his wind the heavens were made fair;
his hand pierced the fleeing serpent.

(Job 26:11–13)

But he didn't win without a struggle, for, again on analogy with Marduk, he was devoured by the monster but then managed to burst out of its belly, ripping it apart in the process. Psalm 18:46a proclaims the joyous tidings of the resurrection, "Yahweh lives!" (Cf the Canaanite version: "Aelyon Baal lives!" And that of the Phrygian Attis cult: "Rejoice, ye initiates! For your god is saved!").[2] From the sundered carcass Yahweh constructed the universe as we know it (or, rather, as the ancients knew it): the concave carapace he raised up to form the umbrella-like firmament above our heads. The lower bed of entrails, legs, ribs, etc., he fashioned into the disk of the earth, floating like a raft upon the face of the bottomless abyss where once the Dragons sported. Henceforth, Yahweh would share the divine dais with his Father, either as co-regent or his successor.

This is what we see happening before the eyes of our mind when we read Daniel chapter 7:2–14.

> Daniel said, "I saw in my vision by night, and behold, the four winds of heaven were stirring up the great sea. And four great beasts came up out of the sea, different from one another. The first was like a lion and had eagles' wings. Then as I looked its wings were plucked off, and it was lifted up from the ground and made to stand upon two feet like a man; and the mind of a man was given to it. And behold, another beast, a second one, like a bear. It was raised up on one side; it had three ribs in its mouth between its teeth; and it was told, 'Arise, devour much flesh.' After this I looked, and lo, another, like a leopard, with four wings of a bird on its back; and the beast had four heads; and dominion was given to it. After this I saw in the night visions, and behold, a fourth beast, terrible and dreadful and exceedingly strong; and it had great iron teeth; it devoured and broke in pieces, and stamped the residue with its feet. It was different from all the beasts that were before

---

2. Geo Widengren, "Early Hebrew Myths and their Interpretation" in S.H. Hooke, ed., *Myth, Ritual and Kingship: Essays on the Theory and Practice of Kingship in the Ancient Near East and in Israel* (New York: Oxford University Press, 1958), p. 191. Given the parallels just quoted, we may consider these exclamations as belonging to a form-critical category: the *resurrection kerygma*, whether of Jesus, Attis, Marduk, Baal, or Yahweh.

it; and it had ten horns. I considered the horns, and behold, there came up among them another horn, a little one, before which three of the first horns were plucked up by the roots; and behold, in this horn were eyes like the eyes of a man, and a mouth speaking great things.

As I looked, thrones were placed
  and one that was ancient of days took his seat;
his raiment was white as snow,
  and the hair of his head like pure wool;
his throne was fiery flames,
  its wheels were burning fire.
A stream of fire issued
  and came forth from before him;
a thousand thousands served him,
  and ten thousand times ten thousand stood before him;
the court sat in judgment,
  and the books were opened.

I looked then because of the sound of the great words which the horn was speaking. And as I looked, the beast was slain, and its body destroyed and given over to be burned with fire. As for the rest of the beasts, their dominion was taken away, but their lives were prolonged for a season and a time. I saw in the night visions,

and behold, with the clouds of heaven
  there came one like a son of man,
and he came to the Ancient of Days
  and was presented before him.
And to him was given dominion
  and glory and kingdom,
that all peoples, nations, and languages
  should serve him;

his dominion is an everlasting dominion,
 which shall not pass away,
and his kingdom one
 that shall not be destroyed.

Though the sequence has been repurposed in its present context, made an allegory of God freeing the Jewish people from Seleucids in 165 BCE, it is much older and was one version of the myth of Yahweh's creation by combat with the behemoths. We see a horrifying parade of one sea-monster after another rising out of the sea, apparently corpses floating to the surface. Then one like a son of man erupts from the watery surface, rejoicing in his victory and taking his seat next to El Elyon, as Baal did with El after his victories over the monsters Yamm (the Sea personified) and Mot (Death personified).

We always ask after the probable *Sitz-im-Leben* of the myth (the situation that led to the myth's creation). Even so here: we know from a wealth of ancient Near Eastern texts (most long predating our Bible) that this saga in its various forms served as the script for the Enthronement Festival as part of the New Year celebration.[3] The king (of Babylon, the Canaanite city-states, Assyria, as well as Israel and Judah) was believed to be the earthly vicar of the king of gods. As with a late variant, the Arthurian Fisher King, the king personifies the land. As the one suffers, so does the other; as the one prospers, so does the other. The Enthronement Festival was keyed to the change of

3. Ivan Engnell, *Studies in Divine Kingship in the Ancient Near East* (Uppsala: Almqvist & Wiksells Boktryckeri, 1943); Sigmund Mowinckel, *The Psalms in Israel's Worship*. Trans. D.R. Ap-Thomas (Nashville: Abingdon, 1962); Aage Bentzen, *King and Messiah*. Lutterworth Studies in Church and State. (London: Lutterworth Press, 1955).

seasons. The belief was that, as Nature ran down, out of steam, vegetation withered. Why did this happen? Because of the accumulating weight of the people's sins. And the king was the vicarious bearer of all that bad karma. Sin must be atoned for; Nature must be revived; the king's divine mandate must be renewed. How might it be done? By bringing back the Sacred Time of Creation.[4]

To that end, the current king would play the role of Yahweh (or Baal, Marduk, Asshur, etc.) defeated by the Dragon, then pulling victory from the (literal) jaws of defeat. He would engage in a dance-charade, as if fighting the Dragon, actually a bunch of guys in a Dragon suit, just like in Chinese New Year parades. His "death" is symbolized by humiliation at the hands of the High Priest, who would knock the crown off his head, tweak his nose, box his ears, whereupon the "repentant" king would confess the people's sins. Then his royal emblems would be restored to him. As the crowds cheered, his majesty would ascend the Temple steps. The great doors would creak closed, concealing him from view. Inside, as was believed, the newly reminted king, having symbolically ascended to the realm of the gods, would be shown the Tablets of Destiny, informing him of future events on the schedule, forewarning and forearming him to rule with wisdom. So closely was the king identified with the king of gods, that he could even be called God.

> Thy throne, O God, is forever and ever: the sceptre of thy kingdom is a righteous sceptre. Thou lovest righteousness, and hatest wickedness: therefore God, thy God, hath anoint-

---

4. Mircea Eliade, *The Sacred and the Profane: The Nature of Religion*. Trans. Willard Trask (New York: Harcourt, Brace & World, 1959), pp. 40–43, 58–62.

ed thee with the oil of gladness above thy fellows.

(Psalm 45:6–7)

Eventually, the elite scribes and priests of Judah came together to "reform" Jewish religion and theology. Scholars refer to this momentous event as the Deuteronomic Reform. It would have been analogous to Vatican II, the Ecumenical Councils, or the Constitutional Convention. The last comparison is particularly apt, since the Founding Fathers were set on "creating a more perfect union" of states, only the ancient Jewish theologians were determined to unify the Godhead: they decided that Yahweh and Elyon were actually one and the same. And the other "sons of God"? They were mere angels. When did this momentous event take place? Learned opinions differ. Traditionally, scholars thought it happened in the seventh century BCE. Russell Gmirkin[5] argues it coincided with the compilation of the biblical canon in Alexandria in the third century BCE. Upstart that I am, I place it in Hasmonean times, the mid-second century BCE.[6]

The concept of the Messiah was not untouched by the bold program of theological revisionism. This drive towards strict monotheism necessitated cutting the Messiah down to size. The

5. Russell E. Gmirkin, *Berossus and Genesis, Manetho and Exodus: Hellenistic Histories and the Date of the Pentateuch*. Library of Hebrew Bible/Old Testament Studies 433. Copenhagen International Series 15 (New York: T&T Clark, 2006).

6. For my money, Rachel Elior, *The Three Temples: On the Emergence of Jewish Mysticism* . Trans. David Louvish (Oxford: Littman Library of Jewish Civilization, 2004), has persuasively described the perfect theologico-historical *Sitz-im-Leben* of the Deuteronomic Reform, though she herself does not draw the inference I am drawing. See my *Holy Fable: The Old Testament Undistorted by Faith* (Valley, WA: Tellectual Press, 2017), p. 130.

Sacred King was too much a god, so he was "demythologized" into a pious king of David's line (at least if you were a Judean; Galileans and Samaritans looked forward to something else, a new Moses perhaps). This king would restore national sovereignty to Israel/Judah. He would rule justly, without wickedness or corruption. He would conquer pagan enemies if needed. He might enjoy a supernaturally extended life span, or he might simply resume the Davidic monarchy, dying when his time should come, leaving the throne to his heir, as Solomon had followed David. But would such a Messiah atone for the sins of his people? No, rather Jews themselves must take care of that. It was up to them to repent. And until they had demonstrated, as John the Baptizer demanded, the fruit of repentance, the Messiah would have to silently wait it out—till the people had proven themselves worthy of liberation. Hence the theological legend that the Messiah was already on earth, albeit in disguise as a leper begging outside the city wall of Rome until one day the news might reach him that the hour had come, that the scales had tipped: enough sinners had straightened themselves out, and it was time to usher in the Messianic Era. It would seem fair to say that so-called Formative Judaism went this way with the Messiah doctrine, while Christians went the other way, retaining the old Sacred King model and applying it to Jesus.

At any rate, you could not simply pull a switch and suddenly have everybody change their beliefs to the new party line. The more drastic the envisioned alteration, the fewer will readily accept them. Even so, it must have taken quite a while for the new theology to take hold in popular belief. Margaret Barker[7] believes that early Christians still made the old distinction between Yahweh and El Elyon. They would have seen Jesus as Yahweh (the Angel of Yahweh),[8] and his Father as El Elyon.

The Red Christ

But I mean to focus on one particular facet of the late-surviving mythology/doctrine of the Sacred Kingship inherited by each successive Israelite and Judean king. They were gods, or as good as gods, and that role was defined as that of a "mighty man of war." Though it seems seldom noticed, the outlines of the Sacred King role quite closely parallel New Testament Christology. The Sacred King was God's Son and God's Messiah (Anointed). See the coronation liturgy of Psalm 2.

> Why do the nations conspire,
> and the peoples plot in vain?
> The kings of the earth set themselves,
>   and the rulers take counsel together,
>   against Yahweh and his Anointed, saying,
> "Let us burst their bonds asunder,
>   and cast their cords from us."
>
> He who sits in the heavens laughs;
>   Yahweh has them in derision.
> Then he will speak to them in his wrath,
>   and terrify them in his fury, saying,
> "I have set my king

---

7. Barker, *Great Angel*, chapter 10, "The Evidence of the First Christians," pp. 190–212.

8. One might fairly say "the avatar of Yahweh."

on Zion, my holy hill."

I will tell of the decree of Yahweh:
He said to me, "You are my Son,
today I have begotten you.
Ask of me, and I will make the nations your heritage,
and the ends of the earth your possession.
You shall break them with a rod of iron,
and dash them in pieces like a potter's vessel."

Now therefore, O kings, be wise;
be warned, O rulers of the earth.
Serve Yahweh with fear,
with trembling kiss his feet,
lest he be angry, and you perish in the way;
for his wrath is quickly kindled.

Blessed are all who take refuge in him.

Let me paraphrase this. It is so familiar to us that we no longer really hear what it is saying.

> Why do the heathen nations waste their time plotting against Yahweh and his Anointed King? All the kings on earth confer together to oppose them. Listen to them scheming! "Now's the time! If we band together, surely we can snap the chains that keep us enslaved!" Little do they suspect that he who is enthroned up in heaven's height hears them and scoffs! "Good luck, you poor fools! I have established my king in his palace on Mount Zion, my sacred mountain! Just try besieging *that!*"
>
> Let me proclaim Yahweh's decree regarding me: "You are henceforth my Son. I have sired you this very day! Just ask, and I will give you authority over all nations! The whole earth

> if you wish! Destroy them like a sandcastle for their wickedness; it's for you to decide!"
>
> You heard it, O kings! Wise up! Live up to the responsibilities God has assigned you! Remember, he is watching you and will be quick to punish! Abase yourselves before him, kiss the king's feet, because, if you don't, you might be found dead on the roadside! It doesn't take much to awaken his fury! But may he heap blessings on you if you will trust in him for guidance.

The Old Testament Sacred King atones for his people's sins. He ritually dies, then rises from the dead, even as Yahweh did at the beginning (Psalm 18:46). And, again, like Yahweh, he is a mighty man of war, exactly as Jesus is depicted in Revelation 19:11–16.

> Then I saw heaven opened, and behold, a white horse! He who sat upon it is called Faithful and True, and in righteousness he judges and makes war. His eyes are like a flame of fire, and on his head are many diadems; and he has a name inscribed which no one knows but himself. He is clad in a robe dipped in[a] blood, and the name by which he is called is The Word of God. And the armies of heaven, arrayed in fine linen, white and pure, followed him on white horses. From his mouth issues a sharp sword with which to smite the nations, and he will rule them with a rod of iron; he will tread the wine press of the fury of the wrath of God the Almighty. On his robe and on his thigh he has a name inscribed, King of kings and Lord of lords.

If this was the way early Christians envisioned Jesus in his second advent, does it not imply it mirrors in some way the manner in which they remembered Jesus in his first advent? If the historical Jesus was a precursor to Mahatma Gandhi and Dr. King, how on earth could he wind up depicted as a blood-spattered conqueror? "Hey! Let's give Saint Francis a makeover—as Genghis Khan! Think of the ratings!" But it would make plenty of sense if it happened the other way around, if the historical Jesus was an armed Zealot who later had to be whitewashed for Roman consumption.

Pacifist theologian MacGregor, years ago, tried to work both sides of the street when addressing the question whether and to what extent Jesus reinvented the notion of Messiahship.

> Jesus seems to have accepted and worked upon the universal assumption that the Kingdom would find its outward expression in a theocratic national community. Indeed, if He had not done so, He must have been largely unintelligible. Had He taken over the idea of the Kingdom and read into it a completely other meaning, without having clear indication that He was so doing, He could only have misled His hearers.[9]
>
> Messiahship for Him clearly meant so much more than it did to the average Jew, that the title might seem more likely to be bestowed upon Him by His disciples than appropriated by himself. But this is to reject the entire historical framework of the Gospels, and thereby foreclose our whole discussion. Now, to whatever extent Jesus may have modified, and did modify the conception of Messiahship, of one feature He could not deprive it, without evacuating it of its whole significance and making its claim meaningless to His hearers: and that feature was the national character of the role.[10] "The most important

9. MacGregor, p. 56.
10. MacGregor, p. 58.

> characteristic of His Messiahship, speaking negatively, is to be found in His refusal to fight the Messianic War."[11]

I think he is merely exhibiting the problem, not solving it. The same enigma would seem to arise if we posit that the historical Jesus was a pacifist even though he will return to finish his mission by mass slaughter on the killing fields of the Valley of the Sons of Hinnom. Does the Rider on the White Horse resemble more the Christ or the Antichrist?[12]

---

11. Hans Windisch, *Der Messianische Krieg*, in MacGregor, p. 59.

12. See Henry Kuttner's story "A Cross of Centuries." *Star Science Fiction Stories*, #4 (November 1958).

5 Roman Provenance

Recent years have seen a couple of interesting modifications of the "Zealot Jesus" hypothesis. According to the Roman Provenance Theory, Christianity was a propaganda device concocted by the Flavian dynasty in order to tamp down militant Jewish messianism by promoting a new, pro-Roman, non-violent messianism. This hypothesis is particularly interesting since it appears to dovetail with the Zealot version. It becomes a question of whether the proposed post-crucifixion, counter-revolutionary whitewash was initiated by Christians themselves, as Brandon thought, or by the Romans.

James Valliant and Warren Fahy,[1] based on hitherto-neglected numismatic evidence, suggest that the Roman-friendly Jesus of the canonical gospels represents a thoroughly Romanized version of the new faith redesigned to domesticate formerly seditionist Jesus-messianism. The basic difference is that, whereas Brandon inferred that Christians themselves bowdlerized the Jesus story to cover their posteriors, Valliant and Fahy credit the

1. James S. Valliant and Warren Fahy, *Creating Christ: How Roman Emperors Created Christianity* (Crossroad Press, 2018).

project to Imperial (Flavian) sponsorship.[2]

In effect, Valliant and Fahy have carried this theory farther and in a surprising direction. They see the gospels concerned, as all of them are, with the fall of Jerusalem, its Temple, and its sacrificial system, not as trying to justify divine Providence but rather as justifying the Roman conquest, defending not God but Vespasian and Titus! And here our authors tread eerily close to the case recently pressed with new vigor by Mike Sullivan[3] and others on behalf of Preterism. That is the doctrine (originally set forth by James Stuart Russell[4] in his 1878 book *The Parousia*) that Jesus predicted the end of the age to transpire in the generation of his contemporaries, not centuries or millennia later, and that it would follow upon the destruction of the Temple—*and that this prediction was fulfilled right on time!* The "Second Coming," then, happened long ago and is not to be expected in the future. Did Jesus return without anyone noticing? Well, it was *supposed* to be like the stealthy arrival of a thief in the night, wasn't it?

Valliant and Fahy agree, but they say that it wasn't Jesus himself returning, any more than John the Baptist was a literal return of the prophet Elijah. No, Mark and the others expected readers to grasp that the "second coming" of Jesus Christ was actually fulfilled in Titus' razing of the Jerusalem Temple! This

---

2. A very similar case had been made a bit earlier by Joseph Atwill in his *Caesar's Messiah: The Roman Conspiracy to Invent Jesus* (Berkeley: Ulysses Press, 2005).

3. Michael Sullivan, *Armageddon Deception: The Eschatology of Islam and Zionism, A Biblical Response* (Ramona, CA: Vision Publishing, 2021).

4. James Stuart Russell, *The Parousia: A Study of the New Testament Doctrine of Our Lord's Second Coming* (1883; rpt. Grand Rapids: Baker Book House, 1983).

might seem absurd until you ask yourself why on earth the evangelists would preserve or create a grossly embarrassing failed prophecy for Jesus. It would seem either Russell was right or Valliant and Fahy are right.

The bitter pill goes down more easily once you learn that not only did Josephus declare Titus' father Vespasian (who conducted the Jewish War until he handed it over to Titus to complete) as the prophesied Jewish Messiah, but that so did Rabbi Johanon ben Zakkai! And Romans Tacitus and Suetonius did, too! As scripture had said, the Messiah had come out of the East to rule the nations. Never said he was Jewish. (Similarly, seventh-century Jews were willing to ally themselves with proto-Islamic "Hagarite" Arabs to follow Umar al-Faruq as the Messiah, though he was an Arab, not a Jew.[5]) Titus inherited his father's Messianic status, so both were deemed fulfillments of Messianic prophecy.

Again, this scenario may seem completely outlandish, but it is not. Alexander the Great, having conquered Egypt, tried to make himself palatable to his new subjects by claiming he was the son of their god, Zeus-Amun.

The underlying purpose of the Flavian scheme would have been to throw a wet blanket over the simmering coals of Jewish anti-Roman sentiment by co-opting the religion that had again and again ignited Jewish Zealotry. So they created a kind of "Reform Judaism" whose Messiah (Jesus) praised the faith of Roman centurions, advised Jews to pay Roman taxes and to happily shoulder Roman field packs farther than Roman law

5. Patricia Crone and Michael Cook, *Hagarism: The Making of the Islamic World* (Cambridge: Cambridge University Press, 1977), p. 5.

required of a Jew, and whose real enemies were not Romans but Jews. The latter had cleverly maneuvered the former into crucifying Jesus even though Pilate declared him innocent. No wonder God slew those murderers and gave the vineyard to better tenants. And the Flavians Titus and Vespasian were the weapons of his justice.

Paul was already spreading a gospel that demolished the wall of the Torah that separated Jew from Gentile. Circumcision was no longer needful. Kosher laws were now moot, and Jesus' death had stultified sacrifices. Paul was bitterly opposed by Jewish Messianists like Peter and James the Just who considered him an apostate and an Antichrist. Of course, these hallmarks of Jewish national identity were precious to Jewish militants, and Valliant and Fahy very naturally cast James, Peter, and their faction as armed militants spreading sedition throughout the Diaspora, repudiating Caesar in the name of another king, Jesus.

Is there any solid evidence for the wholesale Roman fabrication of Christianity as we know it? Or is it all simply an interpretive paradigm to re-construe the textual data of the New Testament (not that that's unimportant!)? Valliant and Fahy lay great store by numismatic evidence, plus ancient mosaics and tombstones which copiously display the "trademark" of Vespasian and Titus (ultimately and admittedly borrowed from the earlier Seleucid emperors): the design of an anchor (sometimes a trident) flanked by dolphins or with Flipper curled around the anchor haft. Why is this important? Well, at the very same time the Flavians were minting these coins, Christians widely embraced this symbol for themselves. Christian use continued long afterward, though, as of the non-Flavian Constantine, it was replaced by the more familiar cross. Given the impression, reinforced by movies like *The Robe* and *Demetrius and the Gladiators*, that Rome engaged in unremitting, widespread persecution of Christians, it would seem extremely unlikely for Christians to appropriate for themselves the favorite logo of their persecutors. But it would make plenty of sense for them to use the symbol of Flavianism if the latter supported their religion—having largely created it in the first place.

All told, the case of Valliant and Fahy seems to depend on this coin as if it were the coin the bank officer flips into the newsboy's change box on a *Twilight Zone*[6] episode: against all odds, the tenuously balancing coin remains vertical all day while, inside the building, the man begins to experience telepathy! Somehow the violation of probability has knocked reality akilter! But the moment the man accidentally tips the coin over flat, he loses the ability to read minds. Well, it seems it does not take very much to knock over Valliant and Fahy's coin, only the realization that this need be no more than yet another instance of early Christians co-opting pagan religious symbols and filling them with Christian meanings.[7] It's going too far to take the dolphin and anchor for a Flavian trademark and the Christian religion as a Flavian product. The famous *ichthus* (fish) symbol used by persecuted Christians had already been used by persecuted Pythagoreans to signal insiders to mark "underground" safe houses. Does that mean that Pythagoreans started Christianity? For all we know, early Christians appropriated the dol-

---

6. George Clayton Johnson, "A Penny for Your Thoughts." *Twilight Zone*, February 3, 1961.

7. Slawomir Poloczek, Review of James S. Valliant and Warren Fahy, *Creating Christ: How Roman Emperors Invented Christianity*. Crossroad Press, 2016." *Journal of Higher Criticism*. Vol. 16, no. 1, Spring 2021, pp. 193–197.

phin-and-anchor sigil to hide behind, hoping to avert Flavian suspicions.

It would serve our authors' thesis well if we could accept the genuineness of the notorious *Testimonium Flavianum* of Josephus, contained in his epic *Antiquities of the Jews*. A Flavian partisan actually mentioning Jesus! Valliant and Fahy are willing to accept a trimmed-down version of the precious paragraph, defending the basic authenticity as best they can. Pardon me, but I am fully convinced by recent work on it that Eusebius created it out of whole cloth, as he did the fanciful Jesus and Abgarus letters.[8]

As defenders of the *Testimonium* always do, Valliant and Fahy appeal to Origen's comment that Josephus did not believe Jesus was the Messiah. Doesn't this mean that the copy of Josephus he was reading did at least mention Jesus, even if as a false Messiah like Theudas or Menachem? No, it does not. Origen was well aware that Josephus hailed Vespasian as the Messiah. That would by itself account for Origen's remark.

Again, these authors invoke Josephus' story of priestly intrigues leading to the assassination of "James the brother of Jesus called Christ." Mustn't this be a reminder of an earlier reference to Jesus? They are very unfriendly to Richard Carrier who would deprive them of this toy. Carrier argues, quite cogently to my mind, that Josephus is referring to the regrettable episode in which Ananus wanted the high priesthood for his own evil

---

8. See Paul J. Hopper, "A Narrative Anomaly in Josephus: *Jewish Antiquities* xviii, 63," https://www.academia.edu/9494231/A_Narrative_Anomaly_in_Josephus, and Ken Olson, "A Eusebian Reading of the *Testimonium Flavianum*," in Aaron Johnson and Jeremy Shott, eds., *Eusebius of Caesarea: Tradition and Innovations* (CHS Research Bulletin, vol. 1.0.11), http://chs.harvard.edu/CHS/article/display/5871.

self and murdered his rival James son of Damneus. The news got back to the new Roman procurator who righted things by giving Ananas the boot and naming James' brother Jesus son of Damneus in his place. Carrier shows how this fits the context, unlike a sudden arbitrary mention of James the Just and Jesus Christ.

Valliant and Fahy cannot brook Carrier's suggestion that the epithet "who was called Christ" is a Christian interpolation. There's no manuscript evidence for that! Of course there's pretty much none, pro *or* con, early enough to settle the question. They note the seeming peculiarity of Matthew referring to "Jesus called the Christ" (Matt. 27:17). Why not simply "Jesus Christ"? Do our authors realize that some manuscripts of Matthew call Barabbas "Jesus Barabbas"? If that is the original reading, then Matthew's "called the Christ" makes plenty of sense: Pilate is clarifying which Jesus is which. "Take your pick: Jesus Barabbas? Or Jesus called the Christ?" And that would be the point of the interpolation Carrier posits: a Christian copyist thought, or wanted to think, that Josephus was referring to Jesus Christ and James the Just, so he inserted the specification. But all of this, I think, is beside the point. Valliant's and Fahy's theory does not depend on the originality of either Josephan passage.

How might Brandon's theory fit with that of Valliant and Fahy? There is one very important difference. The Valliant-Fahy theory has it that it wasn't ex-revolutionary Christians who sanitized and pacified a Jihadi Jesus, but the Flavians! The goal in writing the gospels and Acts was not to protect apolitical, purely religious Christianity from Rome by distancing it from still-active radical Christians ("Hey! It's *them* you want to arrest, not us!"). No, the goal was to promote a safe, pro-Roman Christianity to co-opt the radicals. The result would still be just the same as in Brandon's theory.

But in the end, the Valliant/Fahy hypothesis is a superfluous fifth wheel. The Brandon theory explains the rewriting of a revolutionary Jesus as an accommodationist with Rome in what looks to me a more natural manner. We need only recall the striking parallel between the scenario Brandon proposes and the known post-70 reconsolidation of Judaism. The war with Rome had been sparked by one distinctive segment of Judaism: the Zealot insurrectionists. The mainstream factions of both the Pharisees and the Sadducees had long since learned to live with the Roman occupation. The War eliminated (notwithstanding the Bar-Kochba aftershock in 132 CE) the insurrectionist subset of Jews, leaving only the accommodationists. The Romans had no need to fabricate a new type of (non-militant) Judaism; it was already alive and well, and with more staying power. It is quite natural to see post-War Christianity the same way. Well, *Creating Christ* was a Valliant effort, but as futile as the War with Rome.

Atwill's Messiah

The central thesis of Joseph Atwill's book *Caesar's Messiah*[9] is that Christianity began as the opium of the Jewish people, mixed and prescribed for them by the crafty Flavian dynasty. Vespasian, Titus, and Domitian had had their fill of militant Zealotry and Si-

9. Joseph Atwill, *Caesar's Messiah: The Roman Conspiracy to Invent Jesus* (Berkeley: Ulysses Press, 2005).

cariism. They could not bend the Jewish nationalists to their will even after a destructive war that leveled the temple of their God. No amount of torture could make Jewish prisoners deny their faith and call Caesar not only their salad but also their lord. And so Titus Caesar, with the help of his obedient lackey Josephus, devised a master deception whereby Jews should be seduced into worshipping Titus, divine son of the divine Vespasian, without knowing it, under the guise of a fictitious Jesus, divine son of a divine Father. The gospels were composed by Romans (and Roman stooges, including defeated Zealot leader John of Gischala AKA John son of Zebedee) to catechize Jews into this new and false Judaism which, if they accepted it, should also lull them into a soporific pacifism convenient for Rome.

The four canonical gospels and Josephus' *The Jewish War* were designed and composed to be read together and so to reveal to the cognoscenti this secret origin and rationale for the Christian religion. Further, this Flavian Pentateuch, read thus intertextually, should disclose a series of cruel jokes and parodies of the very faith it presented for the consumption of the masses who read them literally. The Flavian aristocrats themselves would have gotten the jokes, especially the rich jest that the fools who fell for their scam religion were worshipping Titus without knowing it. In a cover blurb, Robert Eisenman remarks, "If what Joseph Atwill is saying is only partially true, we are looking into the abyss." And the abyss is looking back at us.

Eisenman's interest in Atwill's proposal is understandable. Eisenman, in his monumental work *James the Brother of Jesus*, was able to show, from an altogether new perspective, how thoroughly pro-Roman is New Testament faith. Compared with the religion of nationalistic Jewish Christianity it must have seemed the foulest betrayal, an overnight devolution of the faith of a messiah who stormed the temple, condemning its Roman lapdog rulers, into a religion advocating obedience to Caesar, paying him his denarius, and accepting Quisling tax collectors as brothers in the faith. Joseph Atwill is attempting to explain how such a Gentile Christianity, seemingly a perverse parody of Jewish messianism, could have come about.

I will return presently to a handful of oddities that Atwill rightly points out, providing tasty food for further thought. But first I want to provide a broad sketch of the sense I think Atwill's theory would make of New Testament phenomena, which is not to say it is the only theory that might account for these features. Picture a religious ethic of conspicuous compromise with the occupying authorities, a gospel that tells its believers not to resist any who confiscate their property, but to pay Roman taxes and to carry a legionary's field pack twice the distance stipulated by Roman law. Imagine a story that blames not just Jews but implicitly nationalistic, messianic Jews for the destruction of their own temple. A story that has the messiah predict that the kingdom will be taken from Jews and given to a more worthy nation. Keep in mind how the preacher of this sect befriends Jews who collaborate with Rome and eulogizes a Roman centurion for having faith unparalleled among Jews. He is declared innocent by Roman authorities but nonetheless is done in by Jewish rulers. Then think of how the predictions of the fall of Jerusalem a single generation later correspond so closely to Josephus' account of the events. When someone suggests that Christianity may have been a "safe," denatured, Roman-domesticated, messianic Methadone to replace the real and dangerous messianic heroin of the Zealots, and that Josephus had something to do with it, it does not sound unreasonable on the face of it.

Now even this much is highly controversial, debatable, and necessarily so. But if we find this much of the premise beguiling, should we go the rest of the way with Atwill as our guide? After all, somewhat similar theories of a Roman origin of Christianity and of Jesus have been proposed by Abelard Reuchlin (whose notorious 1979 booklet *The True Authorship of the New Testament* strikingly anticipates Atwill's at several points), Margaret Morrison (*Jesus Augustus*), Cliff Carrington (who also ascribes the gospels to the Flavians), and Stephan Hermann Huller (*Marcus Agrippa*, etc.). We might find that one of these alternative theories of Roman origins explains many of the same things Atwill's does, and without the disadvantages.

Atwill's theory does have the advantage of accounting for the persistent pro-Roman tendencies of the New Testament, but consider what else it requires us to accept. First, we are to accept a common, if committee, authorship of Matthew, Mark, Luke, John, and Josephus' *The Jewish War*. There is way, way, too much *else* in any and all of the gospel texts that cannot be dismissed (really, neglected) as mere padding, ballast, which is all it would be if Atwill is right. ("All of Jesus' ministry was about the coming war with Rome and was designed to establish Jesus as Titus' forerunner" p. 260.) Are we to dismiss the diverse, systematic, and subtle theological nuances disclosed by Redaction Criticism? Are all the patterns disclosed by Conzelmann, for instance, to be dismissed as optical illusions?

Atwill sees the gospels as black-comedic satires of events in the Jewish War. For instance, when Jesus offers his flesh for consumption at the Last Supper, it is "really" a wink to the reader who is supposed to think of a passage in Josephus set during the

Roman siege, when a starving woman eats the roasted flesh of her own infant. When Jesus offers to make his disciples fishers of men, the line is supposed to sardonically anticipate a wartime episode in which the Romans picked off fleeing Jewish rebels swimming in the Lake of Galilee. He connects widely separated dots and collects sets of incredibly far-fetched verbal correspondences, from gospel to gospel and between the gospels and Josephus, then uses them to create ostensible parallel accounts. Then he borrows names, themes, and intended references from one "parallel" account and reads them into the other, thus supplying "missing" features. Atwill defies the reader to call it all coincidence, working out the math to show such correspondences could never be the product of chance. For instance, "That the wicked man in the Fulvia story can be seen as a lampoon of Paul seems difficult to dispute" (p. 247). Atwill hammers home the "parallel" between Josephus' story of a Jewish matron, Paulina, tricked into sleeping with a deceiver, Decius Mundus, claiming to be Anubis incarnate, on the one hand, and that of the supposed deception of disguising Titus as the god Jesus, on the other. What do they have in common? Josephus says Decius came forward to gloat, revealing the hoax three days later, while the adjacent *Testimonium Flavianum* of Josephus says Jesus was seen alive again three days after his crucifixion. "There is, of course, a difference. Whereas Jesus appears *on the third day* to show that he is a God, Decius *appears on the third day* to announce that he is not a god. [But] It is implausible that something as unusual as two 'third-day divinity declarations' would wind up next to one another by chance" (p. 245). But, as far as I can see, there is no declaration of divinity in either case.

What is the utility of reading the gospels together as pieces of a single puzzle? If each evangelist meant to send the baffled reader in search of other texts with which to harmonize the one he began reading, it might enable us to iron out the contradictions, say, of the Easter stories. First, as per John 20, Mary Magdalene finds an empty tomb. But it is not that of Jesus. Rather she has mistakenly gone to the recently vacated tomb of Lazarus! She informs Simon Peter and the Beloved Disciple that Jesus appears to be missing. The Beloved Disciple plus a third man, simply "Peter," make their way to the tomb. The Beloved Disciple arrives first but lingers for a moment outside the tomb, nearing the opening. Peter has not reached the tomb yet, but *Simon* Peter beats him there and walks past the Beloved Disciple, becoming the first to enter the sepulcher, where he spots the grave clothes cast aside when Lazarus left. At this specific moment, less than the duration of a minute, one must suppose, a second Mary Magdalene and her sisters (whose visit is recorded in Matthew 28) approach and see the Beloved Disciple outside the tomb. They think him an angel descended from heaven, and he tells them Jesus has risen. The women depart, and the Beloved Disciple joins Simon Peter inside, whereupon another party of women, including a third Mary Magdalene (this time from Luke 24), approaches and sees the two men in the tomb. They take Simon Peter and the Beloved Disciples for angels. They leave, and, moments later, so does Simon Peter. As soon as he vanishes, here comes a fourth Mary Magdalene, this one from Mark, and she spies the Beloved Disciple inside the tomb and thinks he is an angel. He tells her and her companions to relate the news to Peter (who has not yet arrived, remember, only the quite distinct *Simon* Peter!). The Beloved Disciple returns home, but soon the other (Lukan) Peter (not Simon Peter) approaches, having heard the report of the Lukan Magdalene. He has brought at least one other man with him, a la Luke 24:24. The John 20:12 Mary Magdalene sees these men inside the tomb and thinks they are angels. Then she turns and sees a mysterious figure standing outside the tomb, takes him for the gardener, and asks him about Jesus, then thinks he *is* Jesus. But in "fact" he is Titus Caesar. The savvy reader (i.e., Atwill) will get the joke: the "Jesus" worshipped by stupid Christians is really Titus. It is all supposed to be "a comedy of errors" a la Plautus.

Atwill hypothesizes that the Flavian jokesters were compiling the gospels-plus-Josephus as a kind of intelligence test, and Atwill implicitly congratulates himself as the only one in history who has ever passed it.

> I would note that the satirical system that unites the New Testament and *Wars of the Jews* can be seen as an exercise in mind expansion, in that to solve the puzzles the reader must learn to think 'outside the box,' so to speak. The authors were making the point that the narrow focus the Sicarii Zealots maintained regarding a few scrolls was a limited and inaccurate mode of thought. The authors seem to be suggesting that only by seeing all sides of a problem can the truth be known. Therefore it is possible that they designed the New Testament as a tool to intellectually uplift the messianic rebels.[10]

> No it isn't.

> It is possible that the authors of the Gospels created them as a sort of educational tool disguised as a narrative about Jesus. The authors may have wished their readers to work through

10. Atwill, p. 225.

> the various contradictions in logic in order to develop their reasoning ability and thus be able to think their way out of religious superstition. They may have wished the Gospels to be seen by posterity as their contribution to the development of reason.[11]

> The point I think the creators of Christianity were making with their use of comedy is that there are unlimited ways to interpret scripture and it is easy for the uneducated to see symbolic meaning where there is none. They made this point by creating the New Testament as an example.[12]

Atwill is an innovative thinker who gives us the gift of a fresh reading of familiar texts. There are indeed surprising parallels between Josephus and the gospels that traditional exegesis has never been able to deal with adequately, but surely the more natural theory is the old one, that the gospel writers wrote late enough to have borrowed from Josephus and did so. Thus, as per Edgar J. Goodspeed, Matthew 23:35 probably confuses the biblical prophet Zechariah son of Berechiah with the revolutionary martyr Zechariah son of Baruch whose death Josephus relates.

Atwill reasons that Jesus' prediction of the fall of Jerusalem plainly prefigures Josephus' account of the actual events, and he infers that both versions (in the future and the past tenses) stem from the same source, Josephus and his Flavian collaborators. Then, he reasons, the Son of Man whose coming was to climax the apocalyptic scenario must be none other than the actual man who did wreak judgment on Jerusalem, Titus. Atwill congratulates the Preterist school of interpreters on recogniz-

11. Atwill, p.167.
12. Atwill, p. 234.

ing that the Synoptic predictions of the desolation of Jerusalem must have been completely fulfilled in 70 CE, with nothing left over for futurist expectation. Here is one of Atwill's most attractive suggestions.

I believe that Bultmann[13] was right that several "son of man" sayings in the gospels referred originally simply to "mankind" in general (e.g., Mark 2:10, 28; Matt. 12:32). In fact, I wonder if they do not retain this non-Christological "Everyman" denotation even in the gospels. Further, I suspect even more of the son of man sayings are intended this way, e.g., Mark 14:21. Perhaps Mark 13:36 ("And then they will see the son of man coming in the clouds with great power and glory.") is another one. If it were, then maybe what we read there *is* a reference to Josephus' account of the end of Jerusalem, heralded, he says, by people beholding in the flame-tinged clouds the forms of battling soldiers and charioteers. After all, the introductory (redactional) question placed in the disciples' mouths concerns the time of the temple's destruction. In fact, if the son of man stands for Titus, this would solve a major puzzle, namely, how could Mark 13 be a *vaticinium ex eventu* if the intention was to predict the personal, apocalyptic descent of Jesus himself before the then-present generation had expired? The temple was indeed leveled right on schedule, but by Titus, not by Jesus in the Sky with Diamonds. But if the "son of man" in question was *supposed* to be Titus, well, then—mystery solved, never mind the implications for Christian eschatology. Of course, this is the interpretation offered by Valliant and Fahy. They appear not to have gotten it from Atwill, the earlier writer, which goes to show

---

13. Bultmann, *History of the Synoptic Tradition*, pp. 28, 131, 150.

that the scientific principle of repeatability applies here, too. In other words, great minds think alike (e.g., Leibniz and Newton, Darwin and Wallace).

Atwill suggests that Mark's story of Joseph of Arimathea requesting the body of Jesus be taken down and given to him comes from Josephus' own experience of recognizing three crucifixion victims as former associates of his and securing Roman permission to have them taken down alive and treated, though only one survived. How similar are the names "Joseph of Arimathea" and "Joseph b*ar-Matthias*" (the historian's full name)! If the gospel story is based on Josephus' story, that would solve the problem of why Joseph seems to have asked only for Jesus, and what happened to the two other "thieves" crucified alongside him. But to posit such a thing, one hardly need envision a committee writing both stories in the hope that the clever reader would connect them (as if doing so would remotely imply some identity between Jesus and Titus Caesar!).

Independent of the work of Theodore J. Weeden, Atwill traces out the numerous striking parallels between the Passion story of Jesus Christ and the Josephus story of Jesus ben-Ananias, his interrogation by the Sanhedrin and the Roman procurator, his predictions of Jerusalem's destruction, and his flogging and eventual death, suggesting the two Jesuses are one and the same. But surely, as Weeden argues, the explanation is that Mark simply borrowed the story from Josephus.

According to Atwill, "the reader needs to comprehend perhaps the most complex literary satire ever written."[14] But I would suggest that Atwill provides us with the most extreme case of

14. Atwill, p. 169.

the Irony Dodge ever applied to the gospels. Nonetheless, he has also contributed numerous fascinating exegetical possibilities, "dreaming dreams no mortal ever dared to dream before." And so great is the range of his observations that one may easily remain indifferent to many of them and still recognize the value of his scholarship promoting the Roman Provenance theory.

Conclusion: Chariots of Irony

The pacifist apologist MacGregor forthrightly admits that, if a Western (Christian) democracy were to publicly repudiate military self-defense, it might foreseeably result in its complete devastation by a foreign enemy nation. But that outcome is not to be despised, for the shining witness it would exhibit would surely win the hearts of the world, and they, too, would beat their nukes into ploughshares. This is what one might call "political snake-handling." He will brook no compromise.

> A nation, following the way of Christ, might feel called upon to adopt a policy of total disarmament...[S]uch a nation must also be willing, if necessary, to incur the risk of national martyrdom by refusing to equip itself against the possibility of aggression. And it may be that the world must wait for its redemption to risk crucifixion at the hands of its possible enemies. It might lose its own national life; but it would set free such a flood of spiritual life as would save the world.[1]

1. MacGregor, pp. 103–104.

Crucifixion? Well, if it was good enough for Jesus.... You have to wonder: did MacGregor's proposal require unanimous consent of the population? Such a program might not work anywhere but Jonestown, where they used to have a name for it: "revolutionary suicide."

> For the Christian, if he renounces war, will do so, not because he denies that to react against evil by way of war may sometimes be better than not to react at all, but because he is convinced that to use such methods is equivalent to trying to cast out devils by Beelzebub, the prince of devils.[2]

> The principle that one cannot cast out devils by the prince of devils is not a matter of opinion to be proved or disproved by cleverly manipulating texts: it lies at the very heart of the Christian ethic as proclaimed and lived by Jesus Christ Himself.[3]

This is especially ironic since, in my opinion, MacGregor, with nearly every other interpreter, has got the relevant gospel passages exactly backwards. The saying occurs in two basically identical forms, one in Mark, the other in Q (the source of all gospel material that Matthew and Luke share in common but did not get from Mark). It is the famous Beelzebul[4] Controver-

2. MacGregor, p. 95.

3. MacGregor, pp. 106–107.

4. "Beelzebub" is an accidental substitution for the original reading "Beelzebul." The former means "Lord of the Flies," the name of the Philistine oracle god whom King Ahaziah hoped to consult in 2 Kings 1:2–3. He was named such because ancient seers would receive revelation though the sound of insect-like buzzing in their ears. "Beelzebul," on the other hand, was a prince of demons whose power an exorcist might bind in order to set free the possessed. See William Menzies Alexander, *Demonic Possession in the New*

sy. Here is Mark's version (3:22–27):

> The scribes who came down from Jerusalem were saying, "He is possessed by Beelzebul," and "He casts out the demons by the ruler of the demons." And so he called them to himself and began speaking to them in parables: "How can Satan cast out Satan? And if a kingdom is divided against itself, that kingdom cannot stand. If a house is divided against itself, that house will not be able to stand. And if Satan has risen up against himself and is divided, he cannot stand, but he is finished! But no one can enter the strong man's house and plunder his property unless he first ties up the strong man, and then he will plunder his house.

The Q version is slightly different (Matt. 12:24–27; Luke 11:15–22).

> But when the Pharisees heard this, they said, "This man casts out demons only by Beelzebul the ruler of the demons." And knowing their thoughts, he said to them, "Every kingdom divided against itself is laid waste; and no city or house divided against itself will stand. And if Satan is casting out Satan, he has become divided against himself; how then will his kingdom stand? And if by Beelzebul I cast out the demons, by whom do your sons cast them out? Therefore, they will be your judges. But if I cast out the demons by the Spirit of God [Luke: "finger of God"], then the kingdom of God has come upon you. Or, how can anyone enter the strong man's house and carry off his property, unless he first ties up the strong man? And then he will plunder his house.

Testament: Its Historical, Medical, and Theological Aspects (1902, rpt. Grand Rapids: Baker Book House, 1980), chapter VI, "The Beelzebul Controversy," pp. 174–193.

The central logic appears to be clear: demoniacs are hostages to Beelzebul (or Satan). That's why we call them "possessed." They form part of Beelzebul's collection. They are well and vigilantly guarded by their infernal owner. If you knew about those "possessions" and coveted them for yourself, how could you best go about it? Wouldn't you contrive to sneak into the collector's house while he sleeps and tie him up? Then you'd be free to take whatever you wanted without opposition. That is what Jesus (like all his colleagues) is doing. First you "bind the demon," not only to get him out of the way, but to force him to obey you. Then you make him, grumbling and cussing, lead you to all his treasures. That's how it worked! Had Jesus followed MacGregor's advice, he would have left a lot of dissatisfied customers spitting and snarling!

This all implies a great irony: what Jesus and his group tried but failed to inaugurate, the establishment of the Kingdom of God to replace Rome, was eventually accomplished by Rome itself once they made Christianity the state religion. Was this the disastrous wrong turn that Christian pacifists think it was? Hardly. In fact, the change inaugurated with Constantine's edict of religious tolerance changed very little. As we have seen, the previous centuries had already seen a significant number of Christians enlist in the Roman legions. Granted, anti-militaristic arguments were offered by notable theologians like Origin, Tertullian, and Lactantius, but their picture of Christians refusing to compromise with Caesar is not descriptive, though they often put it that way ("We Christians cannot and will not serve in the army!"), is really *pre*scriptive. They want us to think they are offering us the indicative, but in reality they are dealing in the imperative.

> For the crucial change in the attitude of the Church to the claims of Caesar began, of course, after the conversion of the Emperor Constantine to Christianity in 312. The Faith was now exalted, or debased, into a State religion, and Christians naturally began to look to the State for patronage, and in return became more and more reconciled to Caesar's claims even where these might seem to compromise the New Testament ethic.[5]

This assessment is no doubt quite accurate, but it is in a sense irrelevant to our subject. Christians were already marching with Caesar. Constantine's conversion did not change this.

5. MacGregor, pp. 126–127.

About the Author

Robert M. Price is the author of numerous books, including *The Incredible Shrinking Son of Man* and *The Amazing Colossal Paul,* and has written his own translation of the New Testament. He is also the founder and editor of the *Journal of Higher Criticism* and host of the podcast *The Bible Geek*. He holds PhDs in systematic theology and the New Testament from Drew University. He lives in North Carolina.

www.ingramcontent.com/pod-product-compliance
Lightning Source LLC
LaVergne TN
LVHW090924220826
846271LV00023B/86
* 9 7 8 1 6 3 4 3 1 2 8 6 8 *